Psychology in Action

PSYCHOLOGY IN ACTION

Psychology has a great deal to say about how we
working lives more effective and rewarding: the way
people, how they see us, and our ability to communic
and achieve what we want from a situation. Starting
practice in the classroom, the police station, the su
interviewing room, PSYCHOLOGY IN ACTION loo
everyday working methods and concerns of partic
people and asks: where and how can psychology

BACKGROUND TO THE SERIES

This series is an amalgam of two proposals mad
to The British Psychological Society, one by Antony
and Anthony Gale, the other by John Radford and E
The British Psychological Society's Books and Spe
Group brought the teams together to work out the
of the PSYCHOLOGY IN ACTION series, in conjun
Society's Business and Publications Managers. The
have taken editorial responsibility for the first volume
This first title is edited by Professors A. Gale and A

Fo   ming titles in the same series:

Cc   ing and Helping by Stephen Murgatroyd.
Ed   y Professors A. Gale and A. J. Chapman.

Police Work by Peter B. Ainsworth and Ken Pease.
Edited by Professors A. J. Chapman and A. Gale.

Dentists and Patients by J. M. Pinder.
Edited by Dr John Radford and Ernest Govier.

CLASSROOM CONTROL
Understanding and guiding classroom behaviour

David Fontana

Senior Lecturer, University College, Cardiff

Published by The British Psychological Society
and Methuen
London and New York

First published in 1985 by The British Psychological Society, St Andrews House, 48 Princess Road East, Leicester LE1 7DR, in association with Methuen & Co. Ltd, 11 New Fetter Lane, London EC4P 4EE, and in the USA by Methuen, Inc., 29 West 35th Street, New York NY 10001.

British Library Cataloguing in Publication Data

Fontana, David
Classroom control : understanding and guiding classroom behaviour.
    — (Psychology in action; 1)
1. Classroom management
I. Title   II. British Psychological Society
III. Series
373.11'024   LB3013

ISBN 0-901715-42-5
ISBN 0-901715-39-5 Pbk

Library of Congress Cataloging in Publication Data

Fontana, David
    Classroom control.

    (Psychology in action)
    Bibliography: p.
    Includes index
    1. Classroom management.
    I. Title.   II. Series.
LB3013.F65   1985   371.1'024   85-7167

ISBN 0-901715-42-5
ISBN 0-901715-39-5 Pbk

Set in Compugraphic Mallard
by AB Printers Limited, 33 Cannock Street, Leicester LE4 7HR
Printed in Great Britain by BPCC Wheatons Ltd, Exeter

CONTENTS

For Malcolm Butler in friendship and gratitude

INTRODUCTION

It is important to stress at the outset what this book is not. It is not a review of the literature on research projects carried out into class control. Those who expect to find it crammed with references to other people's work are therefore advised to look elsewhere. References, indeed, are kept to a minimum. The reader who is interested in class control is concerned first and foremost with the practicalities of the subject rather than with a purely theoretical knowledge of who has done what by the way of research.

The book therefore introduces the reader to the kind of considerations that should be kept in mind and the kind of strategies that should be developed if good class control is to be achieved, and aims to apply psychological knowledge to the problems associated with this control. Psychological knowledge helps us to understand why children behave as they do, the part that the school and the teacher respectively play in prompting this behaviour, and the skills and the techniques that the teacher can develop to guide this behaviour into more appropriate and acceptable channels. The book is based upon my own experiences both as a secondary and as a primary school teacher, and upon my more recent experiences as an educational psychologist working with student teachers and with in-service courses for teachers, headteachers and deputy headteachers. I have also called upon my varied experiences up and down the country as an external examiner in the principles and practice of education. Not everyone will agree with all the points made in the book and with all the practical advice that it tries to give. Class control is not a topic that admits of the precision that obtains in other areas of psychology and of teacher education. All teachers and all classes are different, and what works in one context may not necessarily work in all. But the book does try to lay down guidelines which are clearly related to the realities of classroom life, and which will help you to think practically and constructively about your approaches to the issues raised by class control.

Obviously some of the class control problems that arise with older children are different from those that arise with younger ones. The book does, however, set out to span both the primary and the secondary school. You will want to interpret much of what is said into specific applications for the primary or for the secondary school, dependent upon where your professional interests lie. But many of the basic principles to which I make reference apply equally at all levels of school education. Hopefully, after working through the book, you will feel you understand these principles more clearly, and will be more confident of your ability to meet and overcome successfully the challenges to class control. These challenges arise from time to time in the experience of all teachers, whether they be straight out of training or well-established in the profession.

Finally, attention must be drawn to two matters of terminology. The first is that, except where indicated to the contrary, the references to teachers and to pupils throughout the book must be taken to apply equally to males and females. Since there is no appropriate non-sexist pronoun available in the English language, plural forms or the terms 'he or she' have been used, and it is hoped that this has not led to unacceptable clumsiness. The convention of using 'she' for the teacher and 'he' for the pupil (or vice versa) has been rejected on the grounds that it still implies a distinction between the sexes. Since both teachers and pupils include males and females in roughly equal proportions, it is unfair and misleading not to reflect this fact.

The second matter of terminology is that for the most part 'the child' or 'children' have been used when I refer to the school population, since the book covers both the primary and the secondary school, and obviously uniform terminology was therefore necessary. Nevertheless, some people may still find this inappropriate, and consider that a word like 'pupils' or 'students' should have been used throughout instead. It is a strange irony that the words 'child' or 'children' should have a pejorative tone for some. This is not the place to speculate on why this should be. Sufficient to insist that in this book they are used with respect and humility.

Part 1. Causes behind Problems of Class Control

Chapter 1

The Nature of Class Control Problems

This is a book about applying psychological principles and insights to the business of controlling a class of children. Nobody particularly likes the word *control* when applied to the classroom, since it suggests rigidity and teacher domination, but it is not easy to find a workable alternative. Let me make it clear, therefore, that I am not concerned with the business of putting the clock back and reinstating an old-fashioned form of discipline in which the teacher's word is law and the needs and inclinations of the children are given no consideration. When I use the word *control*, I mean simply the process of running an organized and effective classroom, a classroom in which the abilities of individual children are given due opportunity for development, in which teachers can fulfil their proper function as facilitators of learning, and in which children can acquire sensibly and enjoyably the techniques for monitoring and guiding their own behaviours. Such a classroom is one in which both teacher and children are aware of the desirability of certain standards of behaviour, and are able to work co-operatively towards their maintenance. Ultimately, such a classroom is a much happier place for both teacher and children, since it provides opportunities for the teacher to experience professional fulfilment and job-satisfaction, and opportunities for the children to experience the right conditions in which to pursue their work and obtain help with the academic or personal difficulties that arise.

Allied to this, such a classroom is a place in which children can be initiated into the process of assuming responsibility for their own behaviour, and of participating in the taking of democratic and well-informed decisions. Paradoxical as it may at first sound, the better the teacher's control of the class, the better the opportunities for involving the children in the day-to-day running of the classroom and in initiating and sustaining learning activities. The purpose of classroom control is not that the teacher is thus enabled to assert personal authority and status over the children, but to enable one to work towards a situation in which the exercise of such control becomes less and less necessary. As children come to see the need for a degree of structure and restraint in individual behaviours, so they become better placed to introduce that structure and restraint into their own lives and, more important still, to appreciate that through a degree of structure and restraint in appropriate areas the opportunities for individual initiative and freedom of action in other areas greatly increase. Neither the teacher nor the psychologist is in the business of curbing individuality or self-expression. Quite the contrary. They are in the business of specifying the circumstances in which such individuality, on the part of everyone and not simply on the part of the strongest and the most ruthless, can best be fostered and developed.

The kind of classroom control of which I am speaking, therefore, is a control based upon an enlightened understanding of child behaviours, and upon a genuine interest in children and in the fostering of their psychological and academic development. But it is also based upon something else, of equal importance. It is based upon an understanding by the teacher of *his* or *her own* behaviour, and upon a realization that many of the problems of control that arise in the classroom are a direct consequence of the way in which the teacher acts (or reacts) towards the children concerned. Children's classroom behaviour should never be considered in isolation. The child is at the centre of a matrix of interrelated forces, each of which acts as a potential stimulus to his or her own capacity to respond. Many of these forces originate from teachers themselves. Others originate from the way in which the classroom and the school are organized and administered. Without too great a feat of memory we can probably all of us recall injustices under which we felt we laboured as children in school and as children in a particular teacher's lessons. We can all of us remember boredom. We can all of us remember school or classroom rules for which we saw little point. We can probably most of us remember humiliations (real or accidental) at the hands of certain teachers, or being exposed to failure or to wounding criticisms as a result of failure. We can probably remember incidents where the teacher misunderstood what we were trying to say, or misinterpreted our motives for certain kinds of actions. And on a less precise but no less relevant plane we can probably remember certain teachers who irritated us almost beyond endurance with mannerisms or methods of procedure, none of which we felt able to influence except by (surreptitiously or openly) various degrees of non-cooperation.

I am not arguing here, of course, that the teacher is always to blame whatever goes wrong. Or even that the teacher is usually to blame. Many teachers already carry enough professional self-doubts without adding to their burden. What I am saying is that whenever things do not go as the teacher thinks they should (whether that teacher is in the nursery school or at the various other levels of formal education up to and including the university) then the behaviour of both teacher and pupil and not just of the latter must be put under scrutiny. It is well to remember, in this context, that the teacher's own behaviour is the only kind of behaviour that is under the teacher's *direct* control. This behaviour is a tool that the teacher uses in order to bring about desirable changes in class behaviour. And when things go wrong within the latter, we must pause to consider whether they are a consequence of misuse of the former.

Even when it is clear that a particular behaviour problem within the class is a direct consequence of the children themselves, teachers still need to look closely at their own response to this problem. The teacher may not have initiated the problem, but their reaction to it may do a great deal to sustain it or even to make it worse. So the teacher examines closely what is really going on in the interaction that is taking place, and by understanding its nature is able to modify personal responses and thus work towards a more satisfactory resolution of whatever it is that is going wrong.

It must be stressed of course (and I stress this again where appropriate) that self-examination by teachers of their own professional behaviours must not be attended by feelings of guilt or inadequacy. If we always end up feeling badly about ourselves every time we go in for this kind of exercise, then we will tend to steer clear of it or to invent all sorts of reasons to 'justify' our actions. These 'reasons' may leave us feeling a little better about things but will inevitably serve to obscure the real factors that underlie the particular classroom crisis under investigation. Self-examination of professional behaviours is simply a way of establishing, calmly and objectively, what part we ourselves played in instigating or sustaining certain classroom activities, and then of proceeding from this to develop improved strategies of response, as necessary, for dealing with similar eventualities when they arise in the future.

I am talking, therefore, about helping teachers understand

children's behaviours, their own behaviours, and the interactions between the two. And I am talking about helping the teacher develop strategies, based upon this understanding, for rendering classroom control more effective, and thus ultimately more democratic, more flexible, and more closely geared to the real nature of children's psychological needs and propensities. As a first step towards this, I shall take a look at the extent of the problems within the classroom likely to be linked with matters of control and management.

The nature of classroom control problems

Insecurities about their ability to control a class of some 30 (all too often 30 plus) children loom large in the minds of many in-experienced and even experienced teachers. Children in the mass can be a daunting – some might say intimidating – prospect, and the young teacher often has a vision of being confronted with an unruly mob that runs riot in the face of ineffectual attempts to control it, and that offers a varied fare of verbal and perhaps even physical violence on and off throughout the school day. But just how true is this picture? How bad are behaviour problems in most of our schools today? In spite of the publicity given to the more extreme cases by the media, things are not as bad as our worst forebodings suggest them to be. One of the most exhaustive investigations into teacher–child interactions carried out in British schools, by Bill Wragg, indicates that the great majority of classroom problems are of the relatively simple 'stop talking' variety. Wearying for the teacher certainly, but hardly a threat to life and limb. And in a sense only to be expected. Few of us, even as adults, would find it easy to sit through one 40-minute lesson after another throughout the day without giving way to the temptation to talk to our friends, revile our antagonists, or look for opportunities for light relief, particularly at the expense of the persons responsible for keeping us confined to our desks.

It is in the nature of people to be noisy when put together as a group. And the less there is to command their attention and interest, the more noisy they are inclined to become. So there is nothing necessarily unnatural (or hostile) about a buzz of conversation when we put a class of 30 children together. Nor is there even if the noise level gets beyond a buzz. In a sense, it is far less natural to have the children sitting in an atmosphere in which you can hear a pin drop. So although problems of the 'stop talking' variety can be a strain upon the teacher, and can certainly interfere with learning, they are not necessarily indicative of any particular threat to the teacher's professional position. And as we see in due course, there is a range of strategies that the teacher can employ to deal with such problems, and the more perceptive he or she is about the cause of these problems (and about what it is or is not possible to expect from a class of 30 children held together in one room for any length of time) the more likely is this range of strategies to be successful.

But of course various other problems in addition to 'stop talking' do occur with varying degrees of frequency in the classroom, though not all these problems are of equal importance. Nor are they all equally prevalent across the whole age and ability range within formal education. Some of them overlap in obvious ways, and some of them will not even be perceived as problems by all teachers. Remember that within certain obvious limits we all of us differ in how we perceive things. What is one teacher's problem may to another be no more than a minor irritation and to another simply a sign of children's boisterous high spirits. In addition, the way in which we view children's classroom behaviours varies across cultures and across the years. This is well illustrated if we look at a list of misbehaviours – together with the punishments they each carried – published by an American High School back in 1848.

1. Playing cards at school (10 lashes)
2. Swearing at school (8 lashes)
3. Drinking liquor at school (8 lashes)
4. Telling lies (7 lashes)
5. Boys and girls playing together (4 lashes)
6. Quarrelling (4 lashes)
7. Wearing long fingernails (2 lashes)
8. Blotting one's copybook (2 lashes)
9. Neglecting to bow when going home (2 lashes)

Doubtless there were even more serious offences which got the perpetrator close to being hanged, drawn and quartered, but the interesting feature of this list is its total neglect of the child's own interests and needs. The majority of the items on it have nothing to do with education and precious little to do with understanding the real effects of harsh punishment upon behaviour. Is lashing a child for blotting a copybook likely to help towards a love of learning and of written work? Is being lashed for telling lies likely to make a child more truthful or simply a more cunning liar? Is a lashing for playing cards likely to help a child find a more productive way of using free time? And note that in at least one instance (boys and girls playing together) children are actually being punished for doing something that we now regard as of great social and educational value.

We can smile at lists of this kind now, but although punishments are much less barbaric these days, we still run the risk of categorizing behaviour as undesirable or deviant in children simply because it goes against our own prejudices or against our own social habits or against our own professional convenience. And all too often we condemn behaviours in children that would be perfectly acceptable (even desirable) in adults, while at the same time reprimanding them for their general failure to 'grow up'. We do this largely because of our own ever-changing beliefs about the place and function of children in adult society, and because of a mis-understanding of the myriad and subtle ways in which ' the child is father to the man'. This is another reason why I stress throughout the book the importance of understanding the reasons *behind* children's behaviour before stepping in with strategies designed to alter it. A strategy that may be perfectly acceptable for one child may lead to an exacerbation of the problem (or perhaps to deep personal distress) with another. Like successful scientists, successful teachers study closely the relevant variables in any situation, and study equally closely the effect of their own interventions. It is all too easy to make snap assumptions about the motivation that underlies children's activities, and to make equally snap assumptions about the effectiveness of our own efforts to influence these activities. The trouble with snap assumptions is that all too often they are based primarily upon our own prejudices or upon our beliefs as to what ought to be happening or what we would like to see happening. Teachers and psychologists are not necessarily exempt from this. As a consequence we fail to develop the necessary sensitivity towards children, and to develop the necessary objectivity and precision in dealing with their needs and with the problems they sometimes generate.

Age-related differences in behaviour

The age of our children has to be taken into account when deciding the cause of a particular item of behaviour and whether or not it amounts to a problem in the classroom. One way of illustrating this – though the illustration must not be taken too far – is to point out that in very young children (particularly at the nursery and infant school levels) many problem behaviours arise quite simply because the child has not yet learnt the acceptable way of doing things. Sometimes the trouble is that children simply do not know what is expected of them, while at other times they may have some idea of what is expected but be incapable as yet of producing the behaviour concerned. The child simply does not know how to wait one's turn, or ask for things politely, or to keep still or stop chattering. While having no particular wish to do things incorrectly or to annoy other children or the teacher, the nursery or reception class child often genuinely is as yet unable to conform to what is expected.

With older children, however, the problem is less likely to be due to an ignorance of set procedures and an inability to produce the required behaviours than to such things as forgetfulness, a casual disregard of set rules, boredom, social problems with other children, or a deliberate attempt to disrupt the lesson or inconvenience the teacher. Nevertheless, even with older children, we should never overlook the possibility that we (or the school in general) have failed to make our wishes sufficiently clear, or that certain kinds of interactive skills whose presence we take for granted in our children may quite simply never have been effectively taught to certain of them.

What the above illustration shows is that the good teacher is well aware of the need to modify the way in which motives are attributed to child behaviours as children grow older. But there is a range of other reasons why the teacher should see the child's age as an important variable in understanding and coping with problems of class control. We can summarize these reasons as follows:

1. *The nature of children's demands and expectations of the teacher change as they grow older.* In the nursery and infant school children tend to require above all a sympathetic and supportive teacher, who can deal effectively and kindly with their emotional and social problems, and initiate them gently into more formal learning. These needs are still apparent in the junior school, but at this age children come to place increasing emphasis upon the degree of interest and intellectual stimulation offered by the teacher, and upon the extent to which fairness and sound judgement are shown in dealing with any problems that arise. By the time the secondary school stage is reached, children are attaching growing importance to the teacher's subject-knowledge and competence. More able children will even tolerate a quite high incidence of arbitrary or insensitive behaviours in a teacher if he or she is known to have an expert knowledge of the material and to be successful at getting people through

examinations. This is less true of 'non-examination-oriented' children of course, but they too admire competence in a teacher: in particular, the kind of competence that indicates success in handling what they see as desirable areas of adult life, and in instructing them by precept or example in the various skills concerned.

The point here is that teachers who can respond to children's changing needs and expectations as they grow older, or who work only with those age groups whose needs they happen to be able to meet, are far less likely to encounter problems of control than those who enjoy neither of these advantages. The teacher who is kind and motherly or fatherly with young children may have this kindness interpreted as weakness by older groups. And the teacher who understands and can work with the problems of the adolescent may have scant patience with those of the reception class infant. In a sense what I am saying is that children have a concept of the successful teacher which changes as they grow older. The teacher who is seen as approximating to this concept is therefore also seen as being effective, with the result that that teacher will be required to do far less in order to assert and maintain authority.

2. The nature of children's relationships with each other changes as they grow older. In the early years of the primary school children tend to function much of the time as single units. They make friends and play together and certainly copy each other's behaviour. But their allegiance to a particular group of friends tends to be slight, and such groups do not usually develop much in the way of a coherent or enduring structure. Later in the primary school, and in particular in the secondary school and during the years of adolescence, the group becomes increasingly important in the life of the individual child. Pressures to conform to group norms in order to gain acceptance increase markedly, as do the identity of the group and intra-group loyalties. The secondary school teacher is therefore much more likely than the primary to have to contend with problems raised by group behaviours and by such things as rivalries between separate groups within the same class.

3. Children's need for status and prestige in the eyes of the class increases as they grow older. Young children like and need to be thought well of by their classmates, and will be deeply hurt if the teacher sets out to humiliate them in front of the class. But as the child grows older this need intensifies, particularly in adolescence, when the child is seeking to establish a sense of personal identity.

A young child (and classmates) will often forget a humiliation by the teacher if it is followed a few minutes later by teacher praise, but an older child may smart under it for days and weeks to come. This is because young children see themselves as non-adult, and therefore as inevitably subject to adult judgement. Adolescents, however, identify themselves more and more with the adult world and search for some status within that world. For an adolescent, to be humiliated in front of one's peer group is to be robbed of that status and to be lowered in both the peers' eyes and one's own. Small wonder that the adolescent will go to great lengths to re-establish personal status by hostility towards the teacher and by attempting to enlist the support of the rest of the class in this hostility.

4. *Children grow bigger and stronger as they get older.* This point may seem so obvious as to be hardly worthy of mention. Yet in fact it is of great potential importance. A class of 30 adolescent pupils can be an intimidating sight to an inexperienced teacher (and to many an experienced one too come to that), and can lead to a loss of that initial confidence which is an essential element in relating to a class. Teachers who are themselves a little lacking in inches may, through no fault of their own, be at something of a disadvantage here. And since children's voices (particularly those of boys) become stronger as they grow older, equally disadvantaged may be the softly spoken teacher or the teacher with a high-pitched voice.

5. *Generally children are more critical of adult behaviours the older they become.* The older child, as mentioned in 3 above, has a strong sense of being on the point of joining the adult world. Adult behaviours, therefore, become of more interest *as behaviours*, rather than simply as things which may or may not affect one's own affairs. With this greater interest comes greater scope for criticism. Adolescents see the possibilities of the adult world without realizing all the constraints. Thus to an adolescent it often seems perfectly plain that they could make a much better job of whatever task the teacher happens to be tackling, and the teacher's apparent failure or difficulties therefore become fair game for comment, rejection and even derision. This is not confined simply to the teacher's professional tasks, but also extends to taste in clothes and cars, to hobbies and interests, and to choice of wife, husband, girlfriend or boyfriend. As with the first point above, the teacher who can measure up to the expectations of children and escape (or at least be seen successfully to deflect) their implicit or explicit criticisms has a far better chance of establishing real personal authority than the

teacher who is generally held to cut a rather sorry figure most of the time.

6. *Older children are often readier to blame adults for their own failures and disappointments.* With the advent of what Piaget terms 'formal operations' (usually from approximately age 12 onwards) the child becomes increasingly capable of abstract thinking and of the kind of reasoning that goes with it. Often this leads to idealism and an appreciation of the unfairness of much that goes on in the world, and often it also leads to a rejection of authority, which is seen to be failing in its task or acting as a hindrance to ambitions or life goals. Children become much more likely to question and challenge this authority and to express their dislike of it and of the things for which it stands. Not surprisingly the teacher and the school are often seen as prime representatives of such authority and are treated accordingly; particularly so by children who have apparently gained little from their education, have little prospect of being entered for, let alone be successful in, public examinations, and stand little chance of doing well in the job market when they leave school and of enjoying the consumer luxuries to which they are constantly exposed by the media.

7. *Children's concentration span and their ability to tackle theoretical work increases as they develop intellectually.* I referred to the advent of formal operations in point 6 above, and with this advent comes a greater readiness to absorb more formal teaching methods, including teacher talk and the presentation of material in a theoretical form. Before formal operations, the child appears to need far more in the way of practical activities in order to understand the concepts which the teacher is endeavouring to introduce to the class, and is far less able simply to sit and listen while the teacher explains things or outlines new ideas. It is a rough rule of thumb (but a quite valuable one nonetheless) that children can sit and listen to teacher talk for approximately one minute to one and a half minutes for each year of their age. After this time, however interesting the teacher, they tend to become restless and to allow their attention to wander. Thus with 10-year-old children we might talk for 10 minutes, or for 15 minutes if they are very able or the subject is a particularly absorbing one. But for 16-year-olds we might talk for anything up to half an hour. This is not to say that we ought to talk for this long, simply that if we do it well we may be able to sustain interest for these amounts of time. The implication of this for class behaviour is that many examples of 'fidgeting' and

'inattention', particularly in young children, are merely instances of the teacher attempting to talk for too long or attempting to deal with concepts in a theoretical rather than a practical way. The moral is simple. The good teacher ensures that teaching methods are suited to the levels of cognitive development reached by children at that stage in their schooling, and thus avoids many of the behaviour problems that occur when children become bored or unable to follow what is being said.

Are older children more of a challenge?

The majority of the above points tend to indicate that problems of class control become more apparent and more complex as children grow older. Older children can be on occasions a great deal more disruptive and threatening than younger ones, and the kinds of demands they make upon the teacher can place an increasing strain upon teaching skills and upon professional self-esteem and self-acceptance. But it would be a mistake to imply that controlling younger children is necessarily always easier. A highly successful secondary school teacher may quickly be driven to exasperation by the chattering and apparently undirected activities of nursery or infant children, and by his or her patent inability to have any appreciable influence upon events. Similarly a class of bright 11-year-olds, with their constant questioning and boundless enthusiasm might prove something of a handful, day in and day out, to the erudite subject specialist used to handling world-weary young ladies and gentlemen of 17 or 18. Children at all ages require special skills, special interests, and a special kind of patience in the teacher, and the key to successful class control at these various ages lies in an understanding of what really prompts child behaviours and an understanding of the strategies most appropriate in relating to and guiding and directing them.

Ability-related differences in behaviour

This is not the place to enter into an investigation of the nature of human abilities. Intelligence, creativity, cognitive styles, thinking, language, and allied factors are fully explored in relevant specialist texts. My concern is simply with the influence that such variables have upon problems of classroom control. For, just as the nature of these problems changes from one age-group to the next, so they change from one ability level to another. And just as it would be wrong to assume that any one age-group invariably makes more demands upon the teacher's class control skills, so it would be wrong to assume that any one ability level is necessarily always more difficult in this respect than the next. The assumption, for example, that non-examination streams in the secondary school are harder to manage than examination streams does not always stand up to the test of experience. A great deal depends upon what the teacher has to offer these different groups. If a class of examination-oriented children, with high expectations, lose their respect for a particular teacher (for reasons I discuss in due course) then they are likely to make that teacher's life just as hard in their own way as would a class of children with little interest in or motivation towards school work.

As with age-related differences, it may be helpful to summarize the major factors leading to variations in the nature of the problems posed by different ability groups.

1. *Motivation for school work will differ markedly from high ability to low ability groups.* High ability groups tend to take a positive attitude towards school and generally identify with the aims and ethos of the school. They will work hard at even relatively tedious material if they are convinced that it will help them attain good results in tests and examinations and thus assist them in realizing long-term career goals. Lower ability groups on the other hand tend to perceive school much more negatively, and to see many of the activities carried on there as a waste of time. In consequence they will focus attention on material for the most part only if it carries intrinsic interest or has obvious relevance to their lives outside school. By 'relevance' I mean that the material concerned seems to the individual to help with the business of successfully running one's life, whether in the vocational, social or leisure sense. I shall be returning to the notion of relevance from time to time elsewhere in the book since it is an important one within the context of class control.

The teacher's choice of material has a vital bearing upon the ease with which class behaviours can be directed and controlled at different ability levels. The point seems an obvious one, but far too often inexperienced teachers find themselves struggling with a class simply because the material chosen for use with them is woefully inappropriate to their level of competence and of interest. And remember that once a teacher has taught a disastrous lesson or two it becomes increasingly hard to reassert authority in the future. The children have already come to associate the teacher with boredom and irrelevance, and subsequent lessons will need to be extra good to break this association and create in its place a more favourable one.

2. *Different ability levels in children make different demands upon the teacher in terms of personal qualities such as patience and sympathy.* All children work better with a teacher who is patient and sympathetic. However slower learners in particular only flourish with a teacher who is particularly gifted in these respects. By showing a lack of patience and sympathy with the learning difficulties encountered by such children a teacher not only makes these difficulties much more acute, but also risks frustrating and alienating the children. The result is that they are driven to give up on their work and to develop a healthy dislike for the teacher into the bargain.

The reader should not assume that I am saying that a teacher who lacks sympathy and patience is never likely to be successful with less able children. It is part of my thesis in this book that many of the skills and qualities required for good class control can be learnt. Failure to sympathize and show patience with the less able (or with the very young) child often stems from a mistaken belief that the child could do the work 'if he would only try' or 'if she would only listen to what I'm saying'. The truth is that the child cannot usually do the work because it is too difficult at that stage in the form in which it is presented. Either it contains concepts which are not yet understood or it presupposes knowledge which the child does not in fact yet possess. By understanding the real nature of the child's difficulties, and by accepting that the child is not deliberately choosing to be a slow learner out of spite for the teacher, it is possible for most teachers to develop the necessary qualities that are essential to give the help that is needed.

3. *The criteria for success and failure differ from one ability level to the next.* Nothing is more dispiriting and demoralizing for children than constant failure. And few things are more likely to lead to behaviour problems in class. Children confronted with habitual failure will often defend their sense of self-esteem by putting all the blame upon the school and the teacher. Not surprisingly, they will develop powerful feelings of hostility towards them. When working with different ability levels the teacher must ensure that the criteria of success are varied in accordance with what is possible for the children concerned at this particular stage in their development. As a consequence children at each level will experience approximately

the same degree of success, and will be led towards the same degree of acceptance of both their own abilities and of the contribution of the teacher. The teacher therefore must study the children carefully and ensure that teacher expectations are realistically tailored to the level at which they are currently able to work. Once they have experienced success at this level and gained in confidence and become more positive in attitude, then the teacher can carefully prompt them into raising their sights and aiming for work at a higher standard.

4. *The facilities and equipment available for children at different ability levels may differ markedly.* Part of the secret of good class control lies in ensuring that an appropriate environment is provided within which learning can take place. Often, however, although such an environment is not too difficult to achieve with more able children it presents major problems with those who learn rather more slowly. This is not because schools necessarily pay less attention to the slower learners or are less ready to spend money on equipment for them, but simply because such equipment frequently is not available. Take the basic example of books. Although slower learning children are as much in need of stimulation and of interesting reading material as those who learn more quickly, there is a far more limited range of text books and of reading primers available for them. Most teachers are familiar with the problem of older slow learners, with horizons commensurate with their age, forced to struggle along with books that are written for much younger children. This is simply because there is a lack of books aimed at their age-group but with suitably modified vocabularies. Many slow learners lose interest in reading because the books they are likely to enjoy are beyond their reading competence while those they can read are far too juvenile in content for their stage of development.

The good teacher uses discrimination and ingenuity to ensure that as far as possible children are provided with learning tools suited to their interests as well as to their competence. To take the example of reading again, there is a great deal provided by the media suitable for adults with restricted reading abilities, and much of this can be used in the classroom. Travel brochures, popular magazines, and certain newspaper articles provide a better springboard for generating interest in reading (and in other areas of the curriculum) amongst slow learning children than do many of the texts available in schools. And once more the generation of interest proves a key factor in reducing the incidence of disruptive behaviour.

Sex-related differences in behaviour

Girls, it is sometimes said, are easier to control than boys. Figures show that there is less incidence of violent or delinquent behaviour amongst girls and fewer of the learning problems that lead to the failures and frustrations and hostilities to which attention was drawn in the last section. But with changing social patterns and a greater realization that women should be allowed to take their place as equals with men there are signs that the balance may be shifting, if only slowly. One of the disadvantages (mixed in with all the advantages) of removing the injustices visited upon the female sex is that a minority of girls may be taking on the negative male characteristics of physical aggression and anti-social behaviour. This makes it dangerous to generalize too much over differences between the sexes.

In any case, physical aggression and anti-social behaviour apart, such generalizations are always risky and often counter-productive. The abilities and tendencies that girls and boys have in common are of far greater importance from the educational standpoint than those in which they exhibit differences. And such differences are often simply the result of social expectations. Adults expect (and therefore countenance) more boisterous and aggressive behaviour from boys than girls, while expecting (and countenancing) more emotional and dependent behaviour from girls. Not surprisingly, the result is that children tend to develop the characteristics that accord with such social stereotypes and are regarded as unmasculine or un-feminine if they fail to do so.

Teachers may indeed find, in the primary school particularly, that girls are more co-operative and show more interest in helping with classroom tasks than boys, while boys show more interest in outdoor activities and in active pursuits. It may also be true that boys show more inclination for mathematical and spatial undertakings, while girls are better at reading, writing and linguistic skills. But it is not clear to what extent these are a consequence of innate differences and to what extent they are simply a result of differences in upbringing. And in any case the good teacher will attempt to minimize the differences by providing both sexes with the same kind of opportunities and the same kind of encouragement to succeed.

Similarly, in matters of class control the good teacher will not show different expectations in terms of male and female behaviours, and will not use markedly different control strategies. Indeed the teacher who does show obvious variations in dealing with one sex as opposed to the other will quickly incur the charge of favouritism from the less favoured sex, a charge which is likely to be backed up by covert and overt challenges to teacher authority. The good teacher will also ensure that teacher praise is linked with categories of behaviour that are the same for boys and for girls. There is evidence to suggest that in some classrooms teachers tend to direct praise at boys primarily for good classwork, and at girls primarily for good social behaviours. This indicates strongly that boys are given more licence for misbehaving in class while girls are given less encouragement to succeed at academic tasks. Such discrimination is hardly conducive either to good behaviour in boys or to academic achievement in girls.

It is sometimes argued by teachers that girls are more prone to emotional outbursts than boys, and that this can lead to problems of a particularly difficult kind. I say more about emotional outbursts in due course, but again it is probably dangerous to generalize too far. There is little hard evidence on the incidence of emotional outbursts in class, since such evidence is beset with problems of definition and with contaminating variables such as the teacher's own behaviour and the response of the rest of the class. It is fair to say however that at puberty, girls are subject to a fluctuating hormonal cycle that can make emotional control difficult (for example, at times of menstruation). There is little to suggest that this has a particularly negative effect upon their school behaviour, but the sensitive teacher is aware of the need for sympathy and understanding at such times, and therefore is able to lessen the chance of such difficulties in emotional control developing into confrontations or other threats to classroom authority.

Finally there is some evidence to suggest that there are differences between girls and boys on certain personality variables that could have a bearing upon class control. Girls tend to be lower in self-esteem than boys, perhaps due to the unfair discriminations made against women by society, and also tend to be rather more anxious and more inclined to take tender-minded attitudes towards social problems. They may also show more interest in the welfare of young children and babies, and more concern with the feelings of others. This has an obvious bearing upon the points already made as to the need to provide children with teaching materials relevant to their interests if problems of class control are to be lessened. Gender differences in personality and interests also have a bearing upon the discussion of personality factors and class control in Chapter 2.

Socio-economic related differences in behaviour

Just as some teachers prefer working with older children and some with younger, and some teachers prefer working with slow learners and some with rapid learners, so there are differences in teacher preferences when it comes to socio-economic background. In these days of comprehensive schools and large catchment areas the contrast in socio-economic makeup between individual schools is now less than it was, but nevertheless still exists. Some teachers prefer to work with upper SES (Socio-Economic Status) pupils while others prefer to be with those from lower SES homes. The differences between the two groups must not be exaggerated, and one of the prime purposes behind the comprehensive school is to work towards their gradual disappearance, but the fact that teachers do have strong individual preferences in the matter indicates clearly enough that such differences do exist and have a significant bearing upon the teacher's professional tasks. From the point of view of class control, the most important of these differences can be summarized as follows.

1. *Children from lower SES backgrounds tend to be lower in self-esteem perhaps because of their underprivileged environment, than those from upper SES.* As I indicated, for example when discussing sex-related differences in behaviour, levels of self-esteem can have considerable bearing upon problems of class control and I return to the matter in Chapter 5.

2. *The values and standards taught in schools tend to accord more with those taught in upper SES homes than with those taught in lower SES homes.* This means that a home–school conflict can all too readily be set up in the lives of children brought up in lower SES backgrounds. The values and standards to which they are expected to adhere in school (politeness, self-control, honesty, academic success, good speech and bearing, non-violence and the like) may be targets for derision at home, while the values taught at home (and which may in fact appear necessary for survival in the tough environment in which the home is situated) may be the subject of censure and prohibition in school. I must stress that many lower SES homes teach the same values as the school, and teach them very well, but it is fair to say that a child from a lower SES home is *more*

likely to be confronted with a home–school conflict than a child from an upper SES home.

From the class control point of view, this means that lower SES children may be more likely to reject the co-operation, self-restraint and academic industry demanded by the teacher than may upper SES children. At nursery and infant school age this rejection may be less a conscious thing than a confusion and frustration at the school for expecting behaviours which seem quite foreign and at which the children have had no practice. But as they grow older, children may rebel intentionally against the school because the values it tries to teach appear to have no relevance to the life they live outside school. Indeed, the school's values may even seem to be a positive handicap, in the sense that experience has taught them that unless they can be tough and aggressive other folk will quickly take advantage of them.

3. *Children from lower SES homes are more likely to find themselves in low ability groups than children from upper SES homes.* The reasons for this are partly apparent from what I have just been saying. Children from upper SES homes are likely to identify quickly with the patterns of behaviour taught in schools because these accord largely with what is taught at home. Coming from homes that prize academic success, they are also more likely to be motivated to please the teacher and to do well at the tasks the teacher sets. Children from lower SES homes may have none of these advantages, and may therefore be more inclined to make a poor start in school, and to slip even further behind from then on. Things may often be made worse by the fact that they may receive little academic stimulation at home, having nowhere quiet where they can study, and may even be subjected to physical deprivation or active hardship.

Not surprisingly such children, through no real fault of their own, are more likely to present the teacher with class control problems, particularly if the teacher is unaware of the true reasons behind their behaviour, or if there are unrealistic expectations in the teacher's mind as to the speed and the readiness with which children can acquire the standards of conduct that the school is trying to teach.

4. *Upper SES children are more likely than lower SES to practise and understand the importance of deferral of satisfaction.* This upper SES value is so important in the context of class control that it requires to be dealt with separately. Deferral of satisfaction means the ability to put off immediate pleasures and gratifications in order

to be in a position to enjoy such things even more fully in the future. Deferral of satisfaction is inseparable from the notion of academic success. One stays in and works hard night after night and one applies oneself in school in order to do well, pass examinations and get on in life. Upper SES children, who are taught from an early age to save up pocket money in order one day to buy the big things they want, and who are admonished to keep some of their sweets for tomorrow, are better prepared for the demands that are made on them to put off immediate pleasure in school. For these children there is some point in paying attention to the teacher and working through often apparently tedious material since this will pay off in the future, just as saving pocket money has done. Children who have not been introduced to the deferral of satisfaction within the home will find this far more difficult, however, and may tend to act with spontaneous irritation in the face of tedium in school, may tend to talk and laugh as the mood takes them rather than waiting until after the lesson, and may regard homework as a poor reason for not going out and having a good time with friends in the evening.

Culturally-related differences in behaviour

Just as it would be wrong to over-emphasize the influence of differences in children's socio-economic background, so it would be wrong to over-emphasize those stemming from differences in culture. By culture we refer not to the sub-cultural variables prompted by socio-economic factors and dealt with above, but to variables associated with the child's ethnic group and with the behavioural traditions within which this group is located. Obviously cultural variables may overlap with socio-economic ones in the sense that certain ethnic groups may experience more than their fair share of social and economic deprivation. But at the same time they introduce a number of considerations particular to themselves and of potential importance to matters of class control.

The majority of these are well-known and well-documented. But there is sometimes a tendency on the part of the educator to regard them in the nature of a hindrance to the achievement of the school's professional tasks, and therefore to be generally rather impatient with them. Such impatience can have an unsettling effect upon the child, and can lead to resentment and to a variant of the home–school conflict to which I have already made reference. At home children are taught to respect their cultural heritage, while at school it may seem that this heritage is virtually ignored, or regarded as anachronistic and out of place. Unable to reconcile the two approaches, children may identify with their culture and regard school as essentially a threat to cherished beliefs and practices. On the other hand they may identify with the school and thus have to reject their own background and, more importantly, that part of themselves that finds identity and security within it.

Either way, but particularly if the child regards the school as a threat, the home–school conflict is likely to lead to difficulties within the classroom and potentially to problems of class control. In dealing with these problems, the teacher may face the added difficulty that children from other cultures often in any case need special consideration. The way in which they interpret teachers' actions and the demands made upon them may vary in a range of subtle but important ways from the responses of children reared in the home culture. By the same token, teachers must pay particular attention to the way in which they in turn respond to the behaviours of children from other cultures. There are dangers that they may interpret the intentions behind these behaviours as conscious discourtesy or as threatening when in fact the children mean them to be nothing of the kind.

The following is a list of the major culturally-related factors that may have bearing upon problems of interpretation of meaning and intention, and upon potential breakdowns in mutual understanding.

1. *Religious and moral codes of behaviour may be more strict in certain cultural groups.* This applies particularly to children from Moslem homes, where girls especially, in matters of dress and behaviour, have far more constraints laid upon them than do most other children. Schools accept this, as they do the wearing of turbans by Sikh boys, but care has to be taken in a number of sensitive areas nevertheless if conflicts and misunderstandings are to be avoided.

2. *Religious observances and rituals may influence the school behaviours of some children.* A good example here is the month-long Moslem festival of Ramadan, where strict fasting is enjoined during all daylight hours. Children observing Ramadan are more likely to find themselves sleepy and inattentive in class than is usual. And even in our supposedly tolerant times, these and other religious observances may invite teasing from children with different backgrounds, thus leading to strife and disagreements and to problems of intervention and reconciliation for the teacher.

3. *Rivalry and hostility may develop between different cultural groups.* Schools play a vitally important part in ensuring racial harmony in our multi-cultural society, and few people can criticize the way in which they discharge this responsibility. But inter-racial rivalries do surface from time to time, leading to conflict and on occasions violence between the groups of children concerned. More subtly, individual children may be goaded or ridiculed within the classroom for reasons of colour or ethnicity, and the problems that arise in consequence require particularly sensitive handling by the teacher. Responses should be geared primarily towards helping children understand the issues involved and the crucial importance of tolerance.

4. *Children from other ethnic groups may experience language problems within the classroom.* Such problems may mean that they do not understand what the teacher requires of them, and their failure to comply is due therefore not to defiance but to simple incomprehension. West Indian children in Britain are a good example of this. Because English is their first language it is often assumed that they use and understand the language in the way that native English speakers do. Frequently this is not the case, however, and the children find themselves classified as problems when really what they need is more help with their usage of conventional linguistic expression.

5. *The degree to which children from different cultural groups are taught emotional and social restraint may vary.* Certain groups, particularly West Indians, are noted for spontaneous, exuberant behaviour, for example. Such refreshing extraversion may nevertheless disturb teachers, who in their attempts to restrain it may frustrate and antagonize the children concerned, thus escalating a minor inconvenience into a major control problem.

Conclusion

In the present chapter I have discussed behaviours that lead to class control problems and examined some of the variables that must be borne in mind. That is the first stage before proceeding to a discussion of the strategies available for coping with these behaviours. Lest it be thought that I have made class control problems sound too daunting, let me emphasize that this book is based upon the conviction that many of the teacher behaviours essential to good class control can simply be learnt. Like any other skill, they appear mystifying only to the outsider. Once the component elements in a skill are fully understood, and practised, it loses its mystery and becomes simple, and reassuring. Once released from the insecurity that comes from unresolved problems of class control, the teacher is much better able to concentrate upon the real priority of the task, namely helping children to learn and enjoy the things that the school has to offer. The aim of successful class control is not to restrict the opportunities for children's personal freedom, but to increase these opportunities by helping children towards a fuller appreciation of how to gain enhanced benefit from their own behaviour.

References

For work by Ted Wragg and his colleagues see: Wragg, F.C. (ed.) (1984) *Classroom Teaching Skills*. London: Croom Helm.

For self-esteem, and sex differences in self-esteem, see: Fontana, D. (1977) *Personality and Education*. London: Open Books.

Chapter 2

Causes of Problems
I: The Children

In Chapter 1 some of the differences between the class control
problems presented by different groups of children were summarized. I now turn to the psychological factors within children
themselves that can lead to problems. I must repeat the warning that
unacceptable classroom behaviour must not be seen exclusively as
the child's problem created by the child. Even if this behaviour is
extreme, like a sudden outburst of anger, and even if the child is
noted for such outbursts, there will usually be factors in the environment that have played their part in sparking things off. The child
may, for example, have been kept too long at a particular piece of
work; may have been asked to undertake a task that is too difficult
or even one that he or she sees as being beneath them; may have
been annoyed by another child, or by something the teacher has
said. Without necessarily excusing this behaviour, we can see that
it can only be fully understood if we keep in mind not only the
child's own psychological makeup but also the actions of other
people towards him or her. The child is at the centre of a matrix of
interrelated forces, each of which acts as a potential stimulus to the
child's own capacity to respond. So although this chapter is concerned with this capacity, it does not fall into the error of regarding
it as something in isolation from the array of environmental factors
that surround the child going about the tasks of learning.

Behaviour problems as learnt attention-seeking strategies

The need to gain and hold the attention of others appears to be a
general human characteristic, as pointed out by Erik Erikson, for
example, and Abraham Maslow. In the early years of life this
characteristic has definite survival value. Unless the very young can

attract the attention of others to attend to their needs for food and shelter, they die. Later, as one grows older, this need takes a more social form. We need the attention of others not only because they can minister to our physical wants but because they give us other rewards such as friendship and guidance and praise. They help us with the business of living, and make us feel wanted and valued and significant as people. One of the most hurtful things that can happen to us, particularly in childhood, is to be consistently ignored by those around us, particularly when the people concerned have an important role to play in our lives, such as parents or teachers or older brothers and sisters.

Happily, many children learn that it is possible to gain the attention they need simply by being natural and open and friendly. If they want help they ask for it, and experience shows them that it is readily and generously given. They experience a loving and supportive relationship with their family, and when eventually they start school they find that teachers generally relate to them in the same positive and friendly manner. They have learnt, in effect, that the way to obtain the supportive attention of others is to follow a pattern of behaviour based upon what might be termed the socially acceptable principles of mutual respect, tolerance and understanding. As they grow older, these principles become an established part of their interaction with others. Since they have been found to give desirable results, the child comes to build them into value systems and into the strategies used for understanding the social world and for evaluating and responding to the actions of others.

Other children, perhaps particularly those from the lower SES homes to which I have referred, are not so fortunate, however. They find themselves born into an environment in which the necessary attention of others is only captured by aggressive and demanding behaviour. Co-operative or restrained behaviour is ignored. Through a process of trial and error the child comes early to learn that the only way to secure the help needed from others is to shout for it. Since even the angry attention of others is often found to be preferable to being ignored, this frequently leads to violence and to battles of wills. As the child grows older, he or she discovers that the only way to secure things is to demand them loudly enough and to hang on to them once obtained. There are no early lessons in waiting one's turn, in showing consideration for others, in asking nicely for the things one wants. Strategies of this nature, if they chance to appear in the child's behavioural repertoire, fail to produce desirable results, and through the trial and error process come quickly to be discarded and to be replaced by the more aggressive strategies that serve to bring results.

Obviously many children grow up in environments which lie somewhere between the two extremes. Sometimes they find that social behaviour brings results, at other times they find anti-social behaviour is more successful. Sometimes they get what they want by asking for it correctly, at other times they obtain it only by loud demands. To take a simple example, a parent may ignore a little girl while she is playing quietly, but come to attend to her or play with her when she becomes bored or frustrated or angry with a playmate. Unwittingly, what the parent is doing here is failing to reward the 'good' behaviour (by ignoring the child when she is playing quietly) and rewarding the 'bad' (by attending to the child as soon as she becomes difficult). The important point to note is that when we speak of attention in this context we include not only what the parents might describe as pleased attention but also what they might describe as cross attention. The parent might feel that speaking crossly to the child is invariably a form of punishment, and should discourage the unwanted behaviour in the child. Unfortunately this is often far from the case. As indicated earlier, the angry attention of others may, particularly for the child who is consistently starved of attention, be preferable to being ignored. Thus although the parent may be convinced that the child is being 'punished' when sharp words and rebukes are used, this may very well not be so. Far in fact from discouraging the unwanted behaviour, the parental intervention may therefore make it worse, as the child comes to learn that the only sure way of getting a parent's notice and attention is to produce behaviour of this very kind.

The process described here is known as *operant conditioning*. At its simplest, operant conditioning refers to the fact that behaviour which is rewarded tends to be repeated, while behaviour which receives no reward tends to be eliminated. Thus in the case of the child, behaviour which secures parental attention (or whatever else it is which the child happens to want) tends to become an established part of the child's repertoire, while behaviour which is unsuccessful in securing the desired ends tends to disappear from it. The point about operant conditioning of particular relevance to us here is that neither child nor parent may be aware of what is going on. The child is simply learning, at a largely mechanical level, that certain behaviours are successful in obtaining what is wanted, while parents are unknowingly rewarding and thus reinforcing the behaviour in a child which they are actually seeking to eliminate.

Obviously as children grow older they become increasingly able to deliberate upon their behaviour and upon the reactions of others towards them and may now choose deliberately to withhold or produce actions aimed at securing desired ends. They will also start to discriminate more clearly between the different varieties of attention that they are able to secure from others. But early patterns of behaviour based upon operant conditioning are difficult to alter, and by the time children are of school age they may already pose severe problems to those around them. The situation is made worse by the fact that when a child starts school he or she may have anti-social behaviour patterns further reinforced rather than discouraged. This is because the teacher, hard-pressed by other charges, may have little time to watch him or her carefully and respond with attention and praise on those few initial instances of correct behaviour. Instead of 'catching the child being good' the teacher will spend most time 'catching the child being bad', that is in commenting upon and attempting to instruct him or her against unacceptable behaviour. Thus, without realizing what is happening, the teacher may well be reinforcing unwanted activities through attention, and failing to reinforce those wanted activities that the child happens on rarer occasions to produce.

The result of this is that the child becomes ever more firmly located in a mode of behaviour that is contrary to the standards and values taught by the school. Due to this mode of behaviour, the child is likely increasingly (and understandably) to be regarded by teachers as a nuisance and as a disruptive influence upon the work of the class. Since such children will tend to fall increasingly behind in this work, due to an inability to establish a satisfactory relationship with teachers, they may come not only to find school boring and irrelevant but also to discover that the only way to gain prestige and status in the eyes of peers is to make professional life difficult for teachers and for those in authority. The child cannot shine by good school work, so he or she becomes instead firmly identified with bad.

Behaviour problems and failures of attainment

Generally speaking, we tend to work best at those things at which we are successful, and least well at those things where our efforts meet with constant failure. If we think back for a moment to the reference to operant conditioning in the last section, it will be clear that this can be explained by saying that a successful outcome to a particular piece of behaviour acts as a reward, while an unsuccessful outcome has the opposite effect. Behaviour that is rewarded tends to be repeated and to become associated in the individual's mind with pleasure and positive emotions, while behaviour that goes un- rewarded tends to become associated with negative emotions, and to be avoided. If the behaviour concerned happens to be school attendance and school work, then we can see that children who find they perform well in the classroom will come to develop positive feelings about school and about their own abilities and will tend to work hard and co-operate with teachers. On the other hand, children who perform badly in the classroom will come to develop negative feelings about school and about their own abilities and will attend school only under duress and with little intention of co-operating with what goes on there.

Thus many behaviour problems in the classroom are a direct consequence of the negative emotions that children entertain about the whole business of schooling. Repeated failure in the classroom (and I discuss the extent and the reasons for this failure in Chapter 3) leaves children with understandable feelings of hostility and rejection towards formal education, and since these feelings inter- fere in turn with their ability to cope with the new work to which they are being constantly introduced, they tend to fall further and further behind and to experience yet more failure. This is perhaps reason enough to explain some of such children's misbehaviours; but things are made worse by two further related factors.

The first is that since they cannot understand much of the work that is in front of the class, they become bored with it and auto- matically turn to other sources of interest, such as annoying the teacher or classmates.

The self-concept

The second factor, which goes rather deeper, is that constant failure inevitably begins to influence the opinion children hold of them- selves. Psychologists refer to the opinions and ideas we have of ourselves as our *self-concepts*, and stress the important part that these concepts play in our performance, particularly in areas such as school work. Positive self-concepts, which allow us to accept ourselves as people and to value ourselves as competent and effect- ive members of the community, generally allow us to tackle tasks with which we are confronted in a purposeful, confident and realistic manner. Negative self-concepts, by contrast, tend to leave us feeling inadequate and incompetent, and often with a sense of defeatism when faced with the same tasks. Children with negative self-concepts (or low self-esteem as it is often called) will frequently therefore doubt their ability to master new work, even though it may appear to them to have intrinsic interest. The same self-doubt will lead them to set themselves unrealistically low standards and goals, or to find excuses for not trying in spite of the fact that, once again, the task with which they are confronted may hold intrinsic interest for them.

Clearly this negative approach to school work will of itself be likely to spark off behaviour problems, with the teacher becoming increasingly exasperated at the child's negative attitude and the child becoming increasingly stubborn about changing it. But there is more to it than this. In the face of experiences which lower our sense of self-esteem we all of us are prone to become defensive. If I fail repeatedly on a task, I can either accept that this appears to prove I have little ability at it, or I can dismiss the whole thing as the fault of the task itself. For example, I can claim it is making unfair demands upon me or I can dismiss it as not worth doing, or I can protest that I could do it perfectly well if it interested me enough for me to want to do my best at it. Whatever strategy I choose, I am defending myself against the feeling of inadequacy aroused by my failure to perform to a more acceptable standard. I am saying to myself (and to anyone else who happens to be observing my woeful performance) that it is not really *my* fault that things are not going well, but the fault of the task itself (or of the conditions under which I am expected to attempt it, or of the person who was supposed to teach me how to do it, or of anything or anyone else handy enough to take the blame).

Thus children who perceive themselves as failures at school must either accept that this is their own fault and an indication of their lack of ability, or they must cast around to find other culprits external to themselves. Not surprisingly, in many instances they will much prefer to blame the school. The work is boring, the teachers useless, and the whole business a complete waste of time. This rejection of school and of most of the things for which it stands is therefore a defence mechanism set up to protect children from experiences which severely threaten their levels of self-esteem.

Note that I am not discussing here whether it *is or is not* a child's fault that school attainment is unsatisfactory. I am simply indicating the mechanisms thát may, often at an unconscious level, operate to make him or her produce problem behaviours. I have, however, said enough to indicate the undesirable effect that constant failure may have upon the child, and this is a theme to which I return in Chapter 3 and also in Part II where I discuss specific strategies for relieving these problem behaviours.

Inadequacies of personal adjustment and behaviour problems

Low self-esteem, however caused and whoever is to blame, is a problem of personal adjustment. It is not, however, the only problem of personal adjustment which can have a deleterious effect upon the way in which a child behaves in school. I am not concerned in this book with severe maladjustment of the kind that requires special remedial treatment (though some of the issues relating to it are discussed in Chapter 7), but many children who would not qualify for this description nevertheless have important personal problems which confuse and disturb them. Many children, for example, come from broken homes, and may feel insecure and vulnerable. Their need for attention and sympathy may lead them into attention-seeking behaviours of a different order from the ones described earlier in the chapter. They may produce persistent clinging behaviour, making unreasonable demands upon the teacher's time and energies. Or they may start deliberately performing badly in class simply as a strategy for being noticed. Or they may express their feelings of unhappiness or frustration by emotional scenes during lessons, or by over-reacting to the teacher's well-intentioned criticisms.

Other children may, through a combination of inborn temperament and experiences at home, be particularly fearful and anxious in much of what they do. Such characteristics may again leave them prone to emotional outbursts in the class which threaten the teacher's authority, or may lead them into lying or cheating simply through a terror of being perceived negatively by the teacher or of being punished for some misdemeanour. This is one of the reasons why I continue to stress throughout the book that it is important we understand *why* a child is misbehaving before deciding upon what action to take. Two apparently similar misdemeanours, carried out by two different children, may stem from quite different motives and may require different responses from the teacher. This places considerable onus upon teachers, and demands from them high levels of skill. Not only must they recognize what lies behind a child's actions, they must also ensure that these actions are dealt with without giving the class the impression that one child is receiving preferential treatment over another. I return to this problem in Part II, and suggest ways in which it can be handled.

Personal problems in children may also stem from an inability to understand how to relate to an adult or to someone in authority over them. In any personal relationship we look for certain signals from the other person that they are attending to us if we are talking, that they respect our point of view, that they recognize the value of our role in life, that they understand our feelings, and that they see the relationship as one involving mutual sympathy and trust. Where the relationship happens to be between a child and an adult, the child in addition looks for signals from the latter which indicate guidance, fairness, competence and the like, while the adult expects reasonable signals of conformity and co-operation from the child. Through no fault of their own, many children are denied the kind of experiences at home which help them both to recognize the appropriate signals from the teacher and to offer appropriate signals in return. They may in consequence entirely misconstrue the help that the teacher is attempting to offer them, and may in turn fail consistently to indicate to the teacher that they are in need of this help, and do in fact appreciate it when they recognize that it is being given.

The consequence is that teacher and child relate to each other in a consistent atmosphere of misunderstanding. Neither in fact sets out to make life difficult for the other, but the breakdown of communication between them means that each becomes more and more frustrated and angry with the other, until the chances of forging a useful working partnership become slender indeed. This problem is evident at all age levels and is so important that I return to it at length in Chapter 5. In the nursery and infant school, the child seems to defy the teacher's best efforts to integrate him or her successfully into the classroom group, while in the secondary school the child seems (and may even have become by this time) opposed to everything that the teacher tries to do to break down the barriers that appear to exist between the child and the kind of classroom relationship that makes work possible.

Finally in this section, some children may suffer from deep personal unhappiness which leaves them withdrawn and apparently inattentive in class, so that the teacher feels the constant need to reprimand them for allowing their attention to wander from the lesson. Naturally enough, the teacher feels that such children could attend if only they would put their mind to it, while equally naturally the children feel that the teacher is picking upon them and only adding to their misery. The reasons for this misery may be many and various. No fewer than 10 per cent of adults will need in-patient treatment at some time in their lives for mental health problems, and a much larger percentage will visit the doctor's surgery for tranquillizers, anti-depressants and other mood changing drugs. We must not glibly assume that these problems only start to make themselves felt in adult life.

Many of the experiences which children have to face from day to day leave them deeply distressed. They may be subjected at home to constant parental nagging or physical assault. Or they may be bullied or sexually abused by older brothers or sisters. Or they may be exposed to the frightening and profoundly disturbing experience of listening to angry quarrels between parents, with or without physical violence. Or they may feel lonely and unwanted, or con-sistently compared unfavourably with older brothers and sisters.

The mere fact that many children never discuss these problems with anyone, or give little obvious indication of their inner con-fusion and anguish, should not be taken as indication that all is in fact well with them, and that all they need to do in class is to stop daydreaming and turn their attention to more important matters. The reality is that these children may already be feeling the depress-ion and tension that will one day take them into the doctor's surgery and perhaps even into the psychiatric hospital. Children's feelings are every bit as sensitive and every bit as easily hurt as those of an adult. Indeed children are very much more vulnerable, and the fact that they develop strategies to hide these feelings because experience shows them that no one has any patience with them or takes them seriously, is all the more reason why the teacher should make a special effort to understand clearly what is going on and to offer the very necessary sympathy and support.

Social influences upon behaviour

We cannot, of course, separate out personal problems entirely from social ones. The problems discussed in the last section clearly have their origin very largely in unsatisfactory social relationships between the children concerned and those who are responsible for their care. Similarly personal problems may serve in their turn to interfere with satisfactory social relationships, and we enter a vicious circle, with the children becoming ever more alienated from themselves and from many of those around them, and ever more likely to pose the teacher with problems of classroom guidance and control. But it is nevertheless convenient, within the classroom context, to draw some distinction between the two, since certain social problems may be of a transitory nature, leaving no very deep impression upon the children involved, and calling for intervention by the teacher at a social or group level rather than at a personal and individual one.

I refer here predominantly to misbehaviour by the whole class. This may be sparked off by the actions of single individuals, but quickly becomes something in which the whole class, or large sections of the class, are involved. And here we come up against the interesting phenomenon that two parallel classes, apparently similar in terms of ability, background and personnel, may pose apparently very different challenges to the teacher. One class may be co-operative, eager and stimulating, while another may be awkward and morose. Yet a third parallel class may be downright antagonistic, only too ready to seize upon any incident which allows them to show derision for the teacher or for certain hapless individuals within the class itself.

What is it that prompts differences of this nature? To understand this we have to understand something of the dynamics of group behaviour. Social groups, whether they be composed of children or adults, tend to develop an identity of their own based upon certain critical factors. For present purposes the most important of these factors have to do with the emergence of friendship patterns, and with what social psychologists call leaders, stars and isolates within the group. To these, of course, can be added the experiences that the group, as a group, has had with teachers in the past (but more of that in the next chapter). Assuming that two classroom groups are evenly matched for ability, age, sex and socio-economic background, then their respective group identities will, to a marked degree, be determined by the influence of certain key individuals within them.

The *leader* or leaders who emerge naturally from within the group tend usually to be those who in some way can give the group a sense of definition. They usually have qualities that are purposeful and readily apparent, qualities that the rest of the group admire and that give the group direction and cohesion. They may be to do with abilities such as courage, or a facility for providing solutions to group problems, or for putting the general mood into words or for thinking of exciting and entertaining things to do. But whatever they are, they are qualities which the rest of the group wants to share, and which give them vicarious satisfaction or which give them, as group members, enhanced feelings of personal worth.

Stars (who may or may not also be leaders) are people who enjoy a special popularity. This may be due to their prowess in things like sport or fashion or pop music, or it may be through their sense of humour or through their generosity or quick and ready support for those in trouble. The star is liked and admired by the group, and although he or she may not provide the kind of group direction provided by the leader, nevertheless he or she sets a standard for others to copy and also helps to give the group its sense of definition.

The *isolate* is the unfortunate individual who has no friends and who is generally either ignored by the group, or used in some way as a butt for the rest of them. He or she may be laughed at and ridiculed, or be picked upon and bullied. Sometimes, since this may be the only way in which they can be tolerated and made to feel a part of the group, isolates will, if temperamentally so inclined, deliberately make themselves into the class buffoon, always ready to provide an objection of derision and therefore an excuse for disrupting the lesson and perhaps discomforting the teacher.

Sometimes a class may contain more than one leader and more than one star (and of course more than one isolate), and may in consequence tend to break down into two or more sub-groups, each one clustered around its own leaders and stars. Just as the main classroom group will tend to develop group norms and standards of behaviour, to which all group members must adhere if they are to be allowed to belong in full measure to the group, so the sub-groups may also produce badges of group membership.

One sub-group may be identified with the teacher and with the work ethos, admitting to membership only those people who are inclined to work hard, while another may be identified with a general rejection of the school and its values, and may be openly hostile (and actively discouraging) to any child who attempts to co-operate with the teacher. Sometimes the whole class will be identified with the work ethos, making isolates of those children who are unable or unwilling to keep up, while sometimes the class will be identified with the anti-work ethos, this time isolating those few children brave enough or anxious enough to want to do as the teacher instructs.

Thus two parallel classes, depending largely upon the orientations of the children in their midst who happen to have the necessary leadership and star qualities, may differ from each other in all kinds of subtle (and not so subtle) ways. I am not suggesting, of course, that leaders and stars are the only influence upon the class, nor that a leader or star could often radically change the character of a class. Children who are too disparate from the rest of the class, however strong their basic leadership or star qualities, are in any case not likely to be accepted as leaders or stars. Thus a disruptive child is unlikely to become a leader in a work-oriented class, and a hard worker is unlikely to become a leader in a disruptive class. Similarly a child who is very significantly above or below the norm of intelligence within a particular class is unlikely to become a leader, and girls may find it harder to become leaders in a co-educational class than boys.

Nevertheless the influence, for better or worse, of leaders and stars upon a class must not be minimized, and it is only by understanding something of the operation of group dynamics that the teacher can develop strategies for dealing with unwanted whole-class behaviours, and for re-shaping and re-orienting the general class attitude to work. Once a teacher is able to identify clearly what is going on within a class, and where the main group influences are coming from, he or she possesses vital information for increasing the effectiveness of the relationship with the class and for intervention strategies in times of trouble.

Limit testing and the growth of independence

Childhood, we like to insist as teachers and psychologists, is a time for exploration. Children, from the early years through into adolescence and the transition into adulthood, are constantly finding out about the world by experimenting and exploring. Such experimentation and exploration, we insist, is to be encouraged, at least within the limits of physical safety and the legitimate rights of others. Yet in spite of this laudable attitude on our part, we often fail to see that much of a child's behaviour in relation to ourselves and to the adult world in general is also of an experimental and exploratory nature. The child literally does not know how adults will react until things are tried out on them. Particularly when children are younger, even the most careful and explicit warnings as to the consequences attendant upon a particular action may not stop them going through with it, first to see whether the adult means what he or she says, and second to determine just how much these threatened consequences will actually hurt.

The point I am making here is that when children appear to 'defy' us, or to refuse to 'listen to reason' they are in fact often applying the exploratory behaviour that they use in gaining knowledge of the rest of the world. This does not mean, of course, that we have to allow children to carry on very much as they please in order that they gain in worldly wisdom, but it does mean that instead of interpreting their behaviour in terms necessarily of deliberate disobedience, we should look to see what particular attempt at learning is taking place. Thus although we may have to be firm with the child in showing that the consequences of this particular action are not greatly to be desired, and had much better be avoided in the future, nevertheless we are able to do it in as constructive a way as possible and without the negative emotional reaction that follows from a belief that he or she is simply trying to annoy us.

Psychologists usually refer to this process of learning on the part of the child as 'limit testing' and I have more to say about it in Chapter 5. When children move up into a new class for example, or acquire a new teacher by other means, they are naturally anxious to find out as much as they can about this stranger and about what he or she will allow. Introductory talks by the teacher, provided they are short and clear and free from too much overt moralizing, can be a help here (and most teachers are going to indulge in them anyway, like it or not), but children are still left with the question as to whether the teacher means what is said, and as to how quickly he or she gets angry and how they look and behave when they do. And even as the class gets to know the teacher better, there will still be occasions throughout the school year when a certain amount of experimental limit testing takes place – often good humouredly it must be emphasized, and with a readiness to accept the limits once the teacher has made it sufficiently clear what they are.

Just as children test the teacher's limits, however, so they also are engaged in a process of testing their own. Will a particular kind of behaviour go down well with the rest of the class for example? And will I feel good or bad if I stand up to the teacher? And does the fact that I am shooting up physically make any difference to how those in authority react to me? In addition, as children grow older, and particularly as they enter adolescence, so they become increasingly aware of their own rights and their own desire for status. Naturally they wish to take more responsibility for their own decisions, and to be given a taste of that independence which they feel (rightly or wrongly) awaits them in the adult world. The more school and individual teachers deny them this independence, the more strongly they are likely to battle for it, and the more strategies they are likely to try out in an attempt to assert it for themselves. The teacher who is conscious of this, and who is ready and willing to grant children the increased self-responsibility which their development demands, is likely to avoid many of the classroom conflicts that particularly surround the teaching of older children, and is likely, incidentally but importantly, to make a valuable contribution to such children's progress into adult life.

Developmental/cognitive factors and behaviour problems

One of the major problems faced by the teacher as a facilitator of children's learning is that the level at which children are able to think and reason may be different from his or her own. Jean Piaget has advanced a theory of cognitive development that suggests that although cognitive growth in children can be thought of as a continuum, there are nevertheless observable *stages* in this continuum, at each of which the child's ability to understand complex ideas and solve problems shows important variations. Of particular relevance for our purposes, Piaget's work suggests that until on average the age of 12 years (there are considerable individual differences between children) the child finds it difficult to cope with certain abstract ideas. At or about the age of 12, as suggested in Chapter 1, the child of normal development passes from what Piaget calls the *concrete operational stage* into the *formal operational* stage, and is now able increasingly to handle hypotheses and concepts even though he or she may not have had concrete experience of the qualities and elements that they contain. Thus the child can begin to understand an increasing range of scientific ideas, for example, and an increasingly subtle range of concepts relating to judgements and evaluations and discriminations.

Once children have entered the stage of formal operations (and the transition is a gradual rather than an abrupt one, with children often reverting to an earlier stage of thinking from time to time), there is less obvious need for them to be introduced to new ideas through the medium of discovery and activity learning, since they are able to grasp more readily than hitherto teacher expositions and explanations of such ideas. This is one of the reasons why, long before Piaget had drawn attention to what was actually happening in terms of the development of a pupil's thinking, secondary schools tended to be more formal and academic in their approach to the curriculum and to teaching methods.

From the perspective of classroom control, particularly in mixed ability groups, the important factor is that the teacher may have children at different developmental levels. In a first-year comprehensive school class, for example, there will be some children who have already achieved the stage of formal operations, and who will be able readily to grasp concepts with a marked degree of abstraction, while there will be other children who are still at the concrete operations stage and who will find such concepts very difficult to master. Should the teacher be working at the abstract level, therefore, the latter children are likely to find themselves unable to follow important parts of the work, and may therefore quickly become bored and liable to start misbehaving. On the other hand, should the teacher insist on working at the concrete operations level for the benefit of these children, the rest of the class who have achieved formal operations may well find the work too simple, and may in consequence in their own turn begin to present control problems.

The problem, of course, is not something confined to the first year of the comprehensive school. Certain children may never achieve formal operations, and will therefore have difficulty with anything other than fairly simple levels of abstraction throughout their school life. Other children, particularly the more able ones, may attain formal operations while still in the primary school, and may therefore find the work offered in such schools provides insufficient stimulation. Or, if we take the teacher as our variable, it may be that the primary school teacher who misunderstands the importance of cognitive developmental levels will insist on offering young (or less able older) children formal and abstract teaching which presents material in a context which is beyond their ready comprehension. Similarly, though less frequently, a teacher of secondary children may pitch his or her teaching strategies at too concrete and therefore too undemanding a level for the class. Both teachers will quickly be faced with the fact that their inappropriate methodology promotes restless and ultimately resentful class behaviour, with the inevitable consequences.

In addition to the concrete and formal operations stages, Piaget identifies a range of other stages and sub-stages through which children pass before they reach concrete operations proper. But from the point of view of classroom control, the implications of Piaget's work are that the teacher must be informed and sensitive as to the level of thinking at which a child is operating. The assumption must not be too readily made that this thinking is simply an immature version of the teacher's own. The child may in fact be genuinely unable to function at the level of exposition and explanation offered by the teacher, and no amount of repetition or of insistence may be of direct help. If the teacher wishes to capture and hold the child's interest and co-operation, he or she must be prepared to modify this level so that it accords more closely with what is currently possible for the child. This emphatically does not mean that children must only be introduced to simple ideas until they are old enough to tackle something more complex. What it does mean is that the way in which ideas are presented must be compatible with the way in which children at the level concerned are able to integrate them into the structures which they use to comprehend the outside world. We can in fact introduce children to quite complex and advanced concepts, provided that we do it in a manner which is consistent with the way in which at that stage in their cognitive development they are able to understand what it is we are trying to say.

Affective factors and behaviour problems

Affective factors (those associated with emotions and personality) are potentially highly significant influences upon classroom behaviour. Earlier in the chapter I discussed the problems that may be associated with inadequacies of personal adjustment, but there are important personality variables even in the best adjusted child which may also have bearing upon what happens within the classroom.

Extraversion–introversion. One of the most widely known of these is the personality dimension which Hans Eysenck labels *extraversion–introversion*. This dimension suggests that an important area of personality can be thought of in terms of the degree to which we are extraverted (at one extreme end of the scale) or introverted (at the other).

The extraverted person tends to be socially outgoing and express-ive, to welcome new experiences, to seek stimulation and excite-ment, and often to be happiest in an environment where there is plenty of activity and external stimuli. The introvert on the other hand tends to favour inner states of mind, and to prefer a more peaceful environment in which to concentrate on a more limited range of activities, finding high levels of external stimulation to be tiring and even stressful.

The majority of people are neither extreme extraverts nor extreme introverts, and find their place at some point on the dimension between these two poles. Nevertheless, in most people one or other of the poles will tend to predominate, and this will influence the way in which they respond to what goes on around them. Eysenck proposes a biological basis for extraversion–introversion, but whether this is the case or not, there seems little doubt that most people show marked consistency in terms of the qualities concerned, with an observable tendency to move slowly towards increased introversion from adolescence onwards.

Within the context of the classroom, extraverted children will, by definition, tend to prefer an environment in which there is plenty of social interaction and social activity, and will tolerate quite high levels of noise and disruption without necessarily allowing it to interfere with their learning. Boredom may set in quickly in a carefully ordered and structured classroom, in which there is little unpredictability and in which the teacher insists upon quiet and static working conditions. Introverted children by contrast, may find a very lively and active working environment, with constant interruptions and new experiences, to be disrupting and unhelpful. They will tend to prefer a classroom in which individual work becomes possible, and in which they are each able to concentrate more upon their own thoughts and their own immediate learning conditions.

What I am saying here is that children, like adults, differ in the kind of setting in which they prefer to operate. Since the classroom cannot offer a range of such settings, and since the teacher will in any case tend to offer the setting which he or she prefers, some children inevitably will find themeselves under-stimulated and bored by it, while other children will find it over-intrusive and unsettling. The usual pattern obtaining in schools is that primary children are given a learning environment based more upon activity and experience, while secondary school children are given an environment which tends towards the formal and structured, and in which the emphasis is allowed to shift away from group and towards more individual work. This is reasonable in itself, and accords with the general shift towards formal operations and towards introversion in children as they grow older, to both of which I have already referred. But nevertheless there are many introverted children in the primary school and many extraverted children in the secondary, and these children may well find that the traditional patterns upon which primary and secondary schools respectively are run are unsuited to their particular personality needs. These children may well, therefore, pose problems of class control. The extraverted child, irked by a quiet environment and an emphasis upon individual work, may frequently break out into disruptive and challenging behaviour, simply through frustration and through a need to introduce variety, of no matter what kind, into procedures.

At the other end of the dimension, the introverted child may produce sudden emotional outbursts in a highly active and socially interactive classroom, as the strains of too much stimulation prove more than can be handled. Or alternatively the introvert may prove stubborn and uncooperative when called upon to take part in activities or to work closely with others.

Since the teacher cannot please children at both ends of the dimension simultaneously unless lucky enough to have a specially designed classroom, he or she may inevitably find that the best solution is a form of compromise, with some lessons or parts of the lesson offering extraverted activities, and others offering introverted. Once a balance is achieved, most children are able to tolerate conditions that are not exactly to their liking, knowing that the teacher understands their preferences and that these conditions will alternate with others that are most suited to their inclinations. Similarly it is also helpful (and reassuring) to children if the teacher is at least able to understand and sympathize with problems that arise from working conditions inappropriate to their particular needs. While clearly unable to allow the kind of disruptive behaviour which I have outlined above, the teacher can nevertheless show a readiness to discuss personal reactions to the way in which learning experiences are presented and to the way in which the classroom generally is run, and a willingness not to insist categorically upon personal preferences in such matters when these are seen to run directly counter to the personality needs of certain members of the class.

Emotional lability (neuroticism–stability). Another of the personality dimensions proposed by Eysenck, that of *neuroticism–stability*, is also of potential importance to problems of class control. Children at the stability end of the dimension tend to be well-adjusted and positive in their approach to life, and beyond the usual boisterousness and limit testing common to most children are not likely to cause significant behaviour difficulties in the well-organized classroom. Children at the neuroticism end, however, in addition perhaps to posing those problems associated with unsatisfactory personal adjustment discussed earlier in the chapter, may have great difficulty in forming effective social relationships with the teacher and with other children. They may be anxious, fearful, suspicious, defensive and secretive. They may find it difficult to communicate their problems and their feelings, and may be unable, through their preoccupation with their own anxieties, to evaluate objectively the intentions and the motives of others towards them. Note that I am not talking here about children who can be classified as having *extreme* behaviour problems (to whom reference is made in the next section), but about children who manage to function fairly adequately for much of the time while finding nevertheless that school presents them with particular emotional difficulties.

The classroom control problems presented by such children tend not to be of the more obvious, directly challenging kind. Some of the children may be poor mixers, and may therefore be isolated and withdrawn, causing the teacher to be more concerned with how to draw them out than with how to quieten them down. This is particularly so where high levels of neuroticism happen to combine in a child with high levels of introversion. However, some children with high neuroticism scores who are strongly extraverted may indulge in persistent attempts at making contact with other children or with the teacher, and may have especial difficulty in coping with tasks that require long periods of individual and concentrated work. As with the extraversion–introversion dimension, Eysenck considers that available research evidence indicates that there is a strong biological determinant behind neuroticism. Some children inherit a nervous system which is all too readily aroused, and which therefore from early life prompts them to feel the symptoms of anxiety much more readily than do others. To this innate characteristic, learning experiences both in and out of school may further contribute, rendering it difficult for the child to gain proper control over a troubled emotional state.

As with the extraversion–introversion dimension, the point I must stress here is that the teacher should be responsive to the child's emotional state, and thus organize class work in such a way that emotional levels are not allowed to rise to the point at which control problems begin to manifest themselves. The practicalities of this are dealt with in Part II (particularly Chapter 6). But with all such practicalities, the most important consideration is to order the classroom in a fashion that largely prevents control problems from arising, rather than simply to apply remedies once they begin to make their appearance.

Cognitive style. Finally in this section, mention should be made of what psychologists call 'cognitive style'. Cognitive style is one of those characteristics which, perhaps as its name implies, contain both cognitive and affective elements. It is in essence the characteristic way in which an individual tends to tackle problems, whether these have to do with social relationships, academic work, or simply the tasks and challenges of everyday life. To take one example. In the reflectivity–impulsivity dimension identified by Jerome Kagan, people can be assigned to positions along a dimension which ranges from the highly *reflective* person at one end, who deliberates carefully before taking any action, to the highly *impulsive* person at the other who typically rushes into any undertaking without pausing to consider the full implications of their actions.

At classroom level, both primary and secondary teachers are all too familiar with children who exemplify these two extremes. Of the two, impulsive children are likely to pose the more worrying problems of class control, though over-reflective children can impose their own particular strain upon the teacher's nerves. The major problem often seems to be that the more an impulsive child is verbally restrained, the more insistent and excited his or her behaviour will often become, as with the children who constantly blurt out answers in class or (in the primary school particularly) leap out of their seats with their hands up in response to class questions. As is seen in Part II, particularly when I come to discuss so-called behaviour modification, there are useful strategies for dealing with behaviour of this kind, but misunderstanding the child's motivation and becoming angry and punitive are certainly not amongst them.

Similar in some respects is the degree of seriousness or non-seriousness with which a child approaches learning tasks. Michael Apter has drawn particular attention to this aspect, and stresses that most behaviours can be undertaken in either what he calls a *telic* or a *paratelic* state. In the telic state, the important thing for the individual is the goal towards which the behaviour is directed, while in the paratelic state it is the behaviour itself that matters. Many people can switch from one state to another as the occasion demands, but others tend to be located in one or other of the states for most of the time. A child located in the telic state will characteristically like to plan ahead and to avoid things which interfere with purposeful activity, while the paratelic child will live for the moment and will welcome diversions and upsets to routine.

Though the notion of telic and paratelic behaviours has implications which reach far beyond cognitive style, the important aspect from the point of view of class control is that the teacher should be aware of which state individual children (or a whole class of children on occasions) tend towards, and also to be aware of his or her own preferences. This information is of value because telic children may, for example, disapprove of teachers who they feel are not sufficiently goal-directed and see them as wasting time, while paratelic children may respond unfavourably to teachers whom they regard as over-serious and purposeful and thus lacking in a sense of fun. In either case, behaviour problems may result. Telic children may become irritated and resentful with a paratelic teacher, and paratelic children may become bored and restless with one who is telic. Successful teachers tend to be people who are not only good at switching between telic and paratelic states as the situation warrants, but who can guide even the more inflexible children into the appropriate state by the lesson material which is presented and by the teaching methods used in its presentation.

Another aspect of cognitive style is *creativity*. Enough has been written about creativity within the classroom and about its measure-ment and encouragement for me to assume an adequate knowledge of these areas in the reader. The point to emphasize is that highly creative children are likely to have an original and individualistic approach to much of their work, which may at times make them uncomfortable members of the class. At times it may seem as if they are being deliberately perverse in the way in which they tackle things, and the teacher may often become exasperated as a con-sequence if he or she fails to understand exactly what is going on. Due to their unconventionality, highly creative children may not be particularly popular members of the class or particularly popular with teachers, and may therefore become something of a focus for various kinds of hostility, discontents and minor rebellions. It hardly needs to be said that this kind of situation is likely to be at its worst in the classroom of a highly conventional and autocratic teacher, and likely to be minimized where the teacher is responsive to individual needs and allows the operation of a due degree of debate and democracy.

The children who pose special problems

The gifted child. Following on from these remarks about the creative child attention must also be drawn to the so-called 'gifted' child. Such children are usually those with levels of intelligence way above the norm for their age (an IQ of 140 +) is sometimes taken as the defining characteristic here), and usually with high levels of creativity and originality in addition. From the perspective of class control, the main problems which they are likely to pose have to do with boredom if the level of work is too far below their ability, and with the degree of challenge which they present to the teacher's professional ego. This last is a less obvious problem than that of boredom, but in many ways it is a more difficult one with which to deal.

Bored children can usually be provided with work at a level more commensurate with their ability, but the child who challenges the teacher's professional ego (or professional self-esteem if you prefer) may provoke a clash of personalities that will persist as long as teacher and child remain in the same school.

Nor is this problem confined to the secondary school, where the child's level of knowledge may be approaching that of the teacher. Even in the infant and junior school gifted children, especially if their giftedness is not diagnosed and acknowledged, may appear to be posing a direct threat to authority, and many teachers may label them as deliberately setting out to be 'smart' or to irritate. They may appear to take a delight in pointing out the teacher's mistakes, or in persisting with a line of argument in direct opposition to the teacher's. Or they may develop their own methods of working and of solving problems, and take care to draw the teacher's attention to the superiority of these methods over those that the latter happens to be offering.

The point about gifted children – and herein lies the threat to the teacher's professional ego – is that they may well be more intelligent and more creative in fact than the teacher, with a much higher potential academic ceiling. Such a situation is not one that some teachers can easily accept, and in consequence they may either try to 'compete' with the gifted child or to repress and punish his or her endeavours. Either way the child is not likely to be easily beaten. Particularly if they come from a home in which their abilities are recognized and encouraged and in which they receive full parental support, they will continue their attempts at self-assertion, often to the further (and public) discomfiture of the teacher. Only by recognizing and welcoming these abilities, and by accepting that the attempts at self-assertion are natural and justified, will the teacher come to terms easily with the child. In doing so, the teacher will learn that far from being threatened by the presence in the class of such an able pupil, professional pride can be taken in the way in which he or she can guide and encourage this burgeoning talent, and make a significant and lasting contribution to what could well become a highly successful or even outstanding career.

The severely disturbed child. A different kind of special problem is posed by the severely disturbed and severely disruptive child. My concern in this book is with what we might call the normal range of classroom control problems, rather than with those associated with extreme personality disorders, many of which may require the attention of teachers specially trained in working with what used to be called maladjusted children (see Chapter 7). Nevertheless most teachers from time to time will find severely disturbed children in the classes they teach, and it is important for them to understand some of the issues involved if they are to relate with any success to the children concerned.

The first point to make is that children who fall into this category, whether in the primary or in the secondary school, do not differ in some fundamental psychological sense from other children. The various factors that have been discussed so far in connection with behaviour problems also lie behind the behaviour of the severely disturbed and disruptive child.

Such a child will often come from a home in which there is little love and support, and in which he or she may witness and be subjected to habitual physical violence. The child may have learnt, largely through the processes of conditioning referred to earlier in the chapter, that the only way to obtain what one wants in life is apparently to be aggressive and show no concern for the rights of others. Disturbed children may have had no opportunity to learn about successful social relationships, and no opportunity to receive or give affection. They may be confused, resentful and hostile, finding it hard to understand the world or to evaluate the motives and behaviours of others. Through the experience of constant failure, they may have come to reject school and everything for which it stands. They may well have been in trouble with the police, they may well have spent part of their lives in care. If they are old enough they may have appeared in court, and they may well belong to peer groups outside school in which the only qualities that are respected are toughness, callousness, and a complete rejection of any extraneous moral code. Since no adult has ever appeared able to understand them or offer them anything they value, they may appear contemptuous towards people who try to help them, to have no loyalty towards such people for their efforts, and constantly to betray the trust that is placed in them.

This sounds a pretty daunting catalogue, and only a small percentage of children will manifest every quality to which it refers. But if it is studied carefully it should become clear that severely disturbed children are the victims largely of circumstances outside their control rather than of any innate viciousness in their own temperaments. Such children literally construe the world in a way that differs sharply from that of most teachers (see Chapter 5), with the result that the chances of genuine communication between the two groups are often minimal.

I must emphasize that I am not seeking to condone in any way the anti-social behaviour that I have just been describing. I am simply indicating that we are not likely to get very far in our efforts to guide such children and integrate them into the rest of the class if we confront them with yet more hostility and yet more attempts at punishment. Having survived in the harsh environment in which they live outside school, these children are hardly likely to be very impressed with the kind of sanctions and threats available to the teacher. On the contrary, they will simply see these sanctions and threats as further proof of the need to wage constant war against anyone in authority if they are to protect their interests and maintain status in their own eyes and in the eyes of their peer groups.

There are strategies that the teacher can adopt for coping with the problems of class control with such children present (see Part II). But for the moment the point to bear in mind is that through an understanding of the reasons behind the way in which such children behave, the teacher will find it easier to be patient in the face of this behaviour. This in itself is a valuable first step towards relating more effectively towards the children concerned. In addition, the teacher will be able to appreciate more fully something of the grimness of the backgrounds against which these children have to grow up, and in consequence will be in a position to identify something of the needs which hide behind their tough and aggressive exteriors.

References

For the work of Erikson and Maslow respectively see: Erikson, E. (1971) *Identity: Youth and crisis*. London: Faber and Faber.

Maslow, A.H. (1968) (rev. edn) *Towards a Psychology of Being*. Princeton, NJ: Van Nostrand.

Group factors and social interaction can be studied in: Aronson, E. (1976) *The Social Animal*. San Francisco: Freeman.

For personality variables see Fontana, D. (1977) or: Fransella, F. (ed.) (1981) *Personality: Theory, measurement and research*. London: Methuen.

Chapter 3

Causes of Problems
II: The School and the Teachers

School organization and behaviour problems

A considerable body of research evidence has been amassed to the effect that the organization, policy and practices of individual schools have important bearing upon children's behaviour. Michael Rutter's research shows that irrespective of children's home background, schools themselves may sometimes be a key factor in determining whether or not certain pupils become disruptive and un-cooperative. The nature of school rules, the system of sanctions and punishments, the accessibility or otherwise of key members of staff, the pastoral care network, the leadership styles adopted by the head and by senior and middle management staff, the attitude towards children's academic and social problems, and the general philosophy and ethos of the school all seem to play an important part in influencing children's reactions.

The school, it seems, that shows a sensitive awareness of the needs of its individual pupils, and that operates in a caring, constructive and positive fashion, is less likely to have problems of anti-social behaviour from children than is the school that adopts a more punitive and less pupil-oriented role.

Before we start wondering how these variables square with a school's academic success record, it must be emphasized that in general the findings of Rutter and others indicate that the school doing well on social measures (such as low delinquency and low truancy rates) also does well on examination results. This holds good even when we compare a group of schools all of which have similar catchment areas. The inference, therefore, is that a school atmosphere which generates good social responses also generates good academic responses. The two go together. This is hardly surprising when we consider that personal–social development and academic development are in fact the two major tasks for which the school is created. The two tasks are not distinct and separate. The one very much supports and informs the other.

Of course it is easier to talk about schools operating in a caring, constructive and positive fashion than to define exactly what is meant by these terms. Much will depend upon the personalities of individual teachers, and in particular on those in positions of special responsibility, such as the headteacher and deputy head-teachers, heads of departments and heads of year. If these key personnel are able to relate well to children themselves, and to provide colleagues with a clear and unified leadership, then the chances are good that the school will operate successfully, even though it may differ markedly in matters of detail from a similarly successful school a few blocks away. Nevertheless there are a number of what we might loosely call organizational features that tend to characterize such successful schools, and these are as follows:

1. The school rules are few in number, but are clear, well-publicized, and consistently applied.
2. Rules are sensible, are related to the needs of the school community, and are seen by the children as being fair and appropriate.
3. Rules, moreover, are subject to change and development in response to the changing and developing needs of the children and of society generally.
4. The school has clear and efficient lines of communication between pupils and teachers at all levels, and equally effective lines of communication between the staff themselves.
5. Decisions taken by the headteacher and by staff generally are never arbitrary, but are related to the procedures, standards and values which the school is seen by all its members to be operating.
6. Where possible, the school provides opportunities for democratic debate on important issues. At the very least, pupils and teachers are allowed to feel that there are opportunities to make their views known within the school system, and that such views will receive sympathetic attention.
7. The school provides effective classroom teaching, related successfully to the children's academic and social goals.
8. The school makes it clear, by word and deed, that it is there to

help children with both their personal and their academic achievement problems. No individual or group within the school is made to feel that they are less important to the community than are any of the rest.

9. The school offers stimulating and adequate provision for cultural, sporting and leisure pursuits, and indicates that these are an integral part of school life.
10. Close and sympathetic links are maintained with the local community, including parents, and full participation by the community in the life of the school is encouraged.
11. There is a set and workable procedure for assessing children with special needs, and for helping them to meet these needs.
12. Children receive clear guidance at points of academic and vocational decision, such as when deciding on options between available subjects, making vocational choices, and preparing for interviews and job applications.
13. The school is seen by pupils of all ability groups to be preparing them for the realistic opportunities and challenges of the outside world, and to be a source of information and guidance in relation to this world.
14. There is an effective system, involving the headteacher and senior and middle management staff, for coping with children who pose particular behaviour problems in the classroom, and for counselling them in relation to these problems.

In addition to these general factors, the curriculum itself can be partly responsible for certain of the class control problems that teachers encounter. Where a curriculum is perceived by children as being of interest and relevant to their needs, the boredom and frustration that lead to disruptive activities are less likely to occur, and longer-term feelings of resentment and hostility towards the school are less likely to develop.

By a curriculum that is interesting and relevant I mean, as was seen in Chapter 1, a curriculum that is perceived by the children as being of value to them in helping them live their lives. That is, a curriculum that teaches them information and skills which help them understand themselves and to relate to others, and which help prepare them for a vocation and also enrich their leisure time. One problem with the curriculum, particularly at the secondary school level, is that it still remains oriented, both in terms of the subjects which it offers and the material contained within these subjects, towards an academic career. Children are given material whose main justification is that it prepares them for further study later on, rather than offering them skills that are of practical or immediate value. There are historical reasons for this, in that originally secondary schools and the curriculum which they developed were thought of very much in terms of preparing pupils for the universities and the professions. With the coming of universal secondary education, few people were able to challenge this thinking, and watered-down versions of the academic grammar school curriculum often came to be adopted for all children, regardless of actual needs.

Matters are changing now, but there is still a reluctance amongst educationists to question the presence of certain subjects on the timetable, and to suggest the introduction of alternatives. Within subjects, both at primary and secondary school level, there is also sometimes a reluctance to question whether certain traditional skills are any longer necessary for children, and indeed whether they may be actually hindering the introduction of more suitable material. The consequence is that many children spend a great deal of time attempting (often half-heartedly and unsuccessfully) to master skills for which they can see little point, while teachers invest a great deal of their energy in what are clearly misguided undertakings.

A radical rethinking of the curriculum, with the introduction of more vocationally oriented and life-skills subjects, and with the disappearance of some of the traditional ones, is likely therefore to reduce very considerably the conditions which breed apathy and misbehaviour in the classroom. Some children are interested in an academic education and other children are not, and both groups of children have an equal right to find that school is a place where these differences are recognized, accepted, and catered for. Even for the more academic child, increased attention could well be paid to the intrinsic interest of what is on offer. The notion of simply learning something in order to pass examinations in order to be able to learn something more and go on to further examinations would then become a less prevalent one.

The examination system and problems of classroom behaviour

This brings me to a closely related consideration, namely the examination system under which schools are forced to operate. Such a consideration relates particularly to the secondary school, though we must not forget that in England and Wales some one third of local education authorities still operate a degree of selection at 11+, which inevitably means that examinations of some kind, however well disguised, are taking place. For present purposes, the importance of examinations is first that, almost by definition, they produce failures as well as successes, and second that (at least in the form in which they are most frequently used in our schools) they have tended to foster the academic curriculum which was discussed in the last section.

Take the problem of failure first. It is relevant to point out that to a large measure the educational system in the UK is geared towards producing failures rather than successes. In England and Wales, one child in four leaves school either without a graded pass in the General Certificate of Education (GCE) or in the Certificate of Secondary Education (CSE) or without even having been thought capable of attempting these examinations. And at the other end of the ability range, under one child in five will achieve five or more GCE passes (or CSE Grade 1 passes), and of these only a handful (approximately 20 per cent of those embarking upon GCE Advanced Level courses) will obtain good enough results eventually to proceed to degree courses at universities and colleges. Although the examination system in Scotland is rather different, the overall picture in terms of results is similar. Small wonder then that the great majority of children will go through their school careers feeling that in terms of qualifications they have little to show for the time thus spent. Small wonder that many teachers feel that the task of interesting and motivating children is an uphill one, with few tangible professional rewards for their hard work.

It may be that current attempts to reform the examination system, and to encourage new initiatives in which the schools themselves play a much greater part in deciding what shall be examined and how it shall be done, will modify the present disastrous state of affairs. But certainly as things stand at the moment many children are being told in no uncertain manner that their performance is deemed inadequate by the formal educational system. Part of the problem lies in the fact that the examinations on offer at present are of the competitive variety. In the case of GCE Ordinary Level for example, examination boards determine *in advance* that the pass mark will be set at a level which fails approximately 40 per cent of children. Thus before they even set pen to paper, four children out of every six will be doomed to failure. The rationale on the part of examination boards for this action is that by passing a consistent percentage of children each year, fluctuations in the difficulty of examination papers from one year to the next and in the standards of marking can be ironed out. This is laudable in itself, but the decision as to *how large* this percentage should be is a purely arbitrary one (why 60 per cent and not 80 per cent, for example?). It means that no matter how well the bottom 40 per cent actually do, they will nevertheless be deemed to have failed.

Examinations of this kind, which compare the individual's performance with the norm for peers, are called *norm referenced* tests. These are likely in the future to give way increasingly to *criterion referenced* tests, that is, to tests which lay down an absolute standard in theory attainable by all those who complete the course and do the work. But it would be unrealistic to assume that the school will ever be free from the problem of children who are early written off (or who write themselves off) as failures, and who in consequence refuse to identify with the objectives of the school and who are prone in the classroom to look round for ways in which they can keep themselves and like-minded classmates amused.

The second aspect of examinations of interest is the link between examinations and the academic curriculum. The relevant factor here is that in preparing pupils for examination work the teacher is often constrained to adhere to an externally imposed set syllabus. This syllabus prevents the teacher from responding freely to pupils' particular interests and needs, to local and national events that have significance for pupils, and even to his or her own specialist skills and strengths within the teaching subject. Children therefore quickly gain the impression that classwork is carried out in the service of the examination syllabus rather than in the service of the people who go to make up the school, and that the ability to obtain good marks rather than the ability to derive enjoyment from school is what counts. I stress in Part II that the ability to capture and hold children's interest is the major strategy available to the teacher in the task of maintaining satisfactory levels of class control, and this implies being responsive to the directions in which sometimes the children wish to point the lesson. The teacher who has to adhere doggedly, come what may, to the set syllabus on all occasions is unable to be responsive in this way. This does not mean, of course, that teachers should allow themselves to be deflected from the main purpose of the lesson every time the children take it into their heads to introduce a diversion, but simply that they should see the lesson as an interactive process in which children, teacher and subject are all allowed to play their full part.

The problem of interesting and involving both examination-oriented and non-examination-oriented children may on the face of it appear less apparent higher up the secondary school, where children are divided up into examination and non-examination streams, and teachers can therefore gear themselves more closely to children's needs. But a school is a community and not a set of separate and isolated classes. Children certainly benefit from being placed in groups according to their abilities and interests, at least in certain of their subjects, but movement between these groups becomes difficult for both children and teachers once examination work is underway. Thus it becomes hard to move individual children to a more advanced group during the school year even though their interests and abilities in the subject concerned may show sudden and rapid development. Similarly it is not easy to move children to a less demanding group if they find difficulty in keeping up. Nor is it easy to convince children not engaged on examination work that they are just as important and just as successful as their examination-oriented peers.

Examinations influence school organization

On a more general but perhaps even more important level, external examinations and the externally imposed syllabuses that go with them, influence the whole way in which a school is organized and structured. Subject specialists tend to be appointed to the staff since they are the people who can prepare children for exams. The academic departments within the school tend to be organized along subject boundaries. Involvement in the community, visits to gain work experience, the teaching of practical skills, all tend to be subordinated to the task of running the school with examination success in mind. And the children who meet with such success tend to become the children who are held up as role models for the rest, just as the teachers who obtain prestige and promotion tend to be those who concentrate upon the more academic work. Note – and this is a vital point – schools themselves can hardly be held to blame for this state of affairs. It would be a brave (or foolish) headteacher and staff who abandoned an emphasis upon examination work in favour of an entirely practical syllabus aimed at the needs of the less academic pupils. The resulting pressures upon the school from inspectors, from the local education authority, and from parents can be well imagined. It would also be an unfair move. Schools have a duty to their able pupils as well as to those who are being failed by the present system. As long as society places such emphasis upon academic examinations taken at the early age of 16 + , schools cannot do other than see to it that their pupils receive adequate help and preparation for these examinations. But while the present policy of failing the majority of our pupils at this young age persists, then schools are, as a consequence, being placed in a situation where problems of bored, apathetic, and disruptive behaviour are almost bound to arise, particularly as children move up the school and begin to see clearly how little they will be able to derive from what goes on within it.

Specific teacher behaviours and class control

I indicated when discussing behaviour problems as learnt attention-seeking strategies at the beginning of Chapter 2 that the teacher may without realizing it be responsible for reinforcing (and thus encouraging) those very behaviours in children which he or she is setting out to restrain. In Part II, I discuss ways in which the teacher can become more aware of this and alter his or her own behaviour accordingly. But in the present section my concern is with the more personal aspects of the teacher's professional performance which may contribute to problems of class control. And here I touch upon somewhat sensitive issues since they have to do in part with the teacher's personality characteristics and self-presentation. Student teachers, in particular, are often disturbed and resentful at the idea that their performance in the classroom may be assessed in part in terms of their personalities ('teacher presence' was the term that once served rather grandly if a trifle imprecisely to cover certain aspects of this area). They often wonder precisely what is involved, and feel justifiably that an element of subjectivity is bound to enter into the judgement of the teaching practice supervisor. Nevertheless, if we think back to our own school days, there is no denying that some teachers seemed to have little trouble in maintaining appropriate class control simply because of their qualities as people, while other teachers struggled hard but unavailingly to overcome defects which seemed to lie in themselves rather than in the material which they had available or the teaching techniques which they chose to employ.

If the remembrance of these classroom battles leaves the reader feeling somewhat intimidated lest he or she too suffers from these same defects, let me hasten to say that what psychologists call rather loosely the 'personality' is not an immutable, inborn quality that we can do very little about. Certain aspects of the personality are undoubtedly susceptible to change and development, indeed the psychologist is very much in the business of telling people how such change and development can best be fostered. So although (to put it at its most brutal) some teachers seem to be marked out as natural victims when it comes to relating to children, in the great majority of cases there is much that can be done to put things right. The first step is always to identify precisely what it actually is about a teacher's personality that seems to invite the worst from children. Is it something that manifests itself in obvious physical characteristics, such as an extreme slowness or hesitancy of speech, or a vagueness in delivery and in responding to children's questions, or annoying mannerisms or habits? Or is it an obvious anxiety, a lack of confidence, a shyness, a diffidence? Whatever it is, it can be identified, and we can then proceed to the second step of finding out why it happens and what can be done to remedy it.

I deal with these strategies in Chapter 7, but I must make it clear at this point that the kind of teacher variables that are under discussion apply in the primary school as well as in the secondary, and apply to teachers of able children as well as to teachers of slower learners.

The notion that a teacher who fails to relate satisfactorily to older children or to those of more limited ability stands a much better chance of succeeding with younger children or with more gifted children is a dangerous error, and one which has been responsible for foisting many an unsatisfactory secondary teacher upon the primary school in days gone by. Certainly primary children, by virtue of their enthusiastic and friendly manner, may seem initially easier to teach than older children, just as a more able class might seem initially easier than a less able one, but in the longer term the qualities that interfere with success in one school or with one ability group are also likely to prove a hindrance in others.

There is no 'easy' option in teaching. Children at all levels have a gift for detecting inadequacies in a teacher, and once detected, these inadequacies are likely to be used as a way of enlivening lessons and as a way of demonstrating the power that children are able to wield over this supposed representative of authority. Children can hardly be blamed for this. For much of their lives they are kept in a position of subordination by the adult world and in particular by the adult world as expressed through the school, and a chance to assert themselves against this world is not to be foregone too lightly.

In addition to personality factors, there is a range of more straightforward and less contentious issues which influence the degree to which a teacher is able to exercise the necessary class control.

Physical appearance is one such issue. Is there something about the teacher's dress or hairstyle that is likely to attract ridicule from the class? Is there an annoying habit of gesture perhaps? Or does he or she pace up and down the room while talking as if oblivious of the presence of the class?; or fail to look at children when addressing them?; or take the lesson slouched in a chair behind the desk? Voice is another important issue. Does the teacher speak too loudly or too softly most of the time? Or mutter or punctuate speech with long pauses and a succession of 'ers' and 'ums' (which the children delight in counting)? Or is the voice monotonous, or accented in a way that is unfamiliar and confusing for the children?

A third issue is related to the way in which the teacher presents the lesson. Is it suitable for the children's ability levels, age and interests? Does it contain sufficient practical work and pupil participation or is it in the form of a long lecture? A fourth issue relates to lesson preparation and organization. Does the teacher have things planned so that the lesson runs smoothly, or do things appear to lurch from crisis to crisis? A fifth issue has to do with the way in which teachers talk to children. Do they show interest and liking for the children, or is their manner curt and dismissive? Do they relate to all the class or simply to the group at the front or to the group that shares their own interests? A sixth issue is concerned with the way in which threats, rewards and punishments are used. Is the teacher seen always to be fair and consistent? Is he or she realistic in what is expected? Has he or she rewards which are valued by the class when awarded? Does he or she place more emphasis upon these rewards and upon encouragement generally than upon blame and accusations?

All these points are looked at in detail in Part II, but I introduce them now to indicate that much depends simply upon the teacher's learning the right skills and techniques. Each of the issues referred to above has far more to do with learning than with factors intrinsic to the teacher as a person. The teacher can learn to restrain physical mannerisms, to control and use the voice correctly, to dress appropriately, to prepare and deliver work correctly, and to be welcoming and positive when relating to children rather than remote or negative. Much of this learning depends upon experience. Courses of initial teacher training and books such as the present one can draw the young teacher's attention to the more important aspects of his or her work, but to this must be added the teacher's own experience with children in the classroom. Only by working with children can the teacher come to understand them fully, and come to modify and develop self-presentation and teaching techniques into a form which are acceptable to children, and which are sufficiently flexible to be responsive to the individual needs of different groups and of different individuals within those groups. But – and this is vital – the teacher must enter upon this experience with a readiness to learn from children and with a determination not to be daunted by initial difficulties.

Classroom organization and problems of control

In addition to the influence which the teacher's personal and lesson organization have upon class control, there are also broader issues which have to do with classroom organization. By this I mean not just the way in which the classroom is physically arranged (children's seating, the availability of essential books and equipment, etc.), but also the way in which the class is administered and the way in which the timetable is structured. To take the timetable first. In the primary school, the individual teacher often has considerable freedom as to when lessons shall be slotted in and as to when one activity shall give way to another. With the exception of lessons like music and physical education, which may require use of common facilities such as the hall, many headteachers are happy to leave timetabling in the hands of individual teachers provided that appropriate allocations are made for each subject and the general syllabus for the year properly covered. In the secondary school this kind of freedom is not possible, but it is important for the secondary school teacher nevertheless to be aware of the influence that the timetable has upon children's behaviour in individual lessons.

At its simplest, most teachers appear to take the view that children work best at the so-called 'basic' subjects before midday, and are ready for freer and perhaps less demanding subjects in the afternoon. Whether this is in fact true of all children is not clear, for people seem to peak in their powers of concentration at different times of the day. But since this kind of thinking on the part of teachers has developed from experience, it may be that generally children are better equipped to handle mathematics and languages in the morning, and art and craft and creative writing in the afternoon. Thus it certainly makes sense for the primary school teacher to start off with this kind of pattern, and then to introduce variations (though not so frequently that the children become confused) from time to time in order to note the effect. If children appear to 'settle' best to certain subjects at certain times of the day, then it makes sense to plan things accordingly.

Timetable planning. For both primary and secondary schools, however, problems often arise when children have to move from one activity to another, irrespective of when this happens. In the secondary school things are further complicated by the fact that often the children have physically to move from one room to another, and have to adjust from one teacher to somebody else. But in both primary and secondary schools, children do not always find it easy to switch their minds from one kind of lesson to another. This is particularly obvious when the children are called upon to go from a physically active lesson, such as physical education, to a sedentary lesson demanding intense concentration, such as a grammar lesson. But it may also be the case when children move from a popular lesson to one that is less well-liked or from an open-ended lesson such as art to a more convergent lesson such as mathematics. Inevitably the result will be a certain amount of unrest, with the teacher becoming exasperated and calling for attention and effort and the children becoming rebellious and calling (albeit *sotto voce*) for the teacher's abrupt demise.

Careful timetabling can often prevent sharp transitions between very disparate activities, though in the large secondary school this may bring the unfortunate individual responsible for the timetable one step nearer to an early breakdown. At the same time, of course, it is undesirable to leave children with a large stretch of the day scheduled for one intellectually very demanding subject after another. A colleague of mine, now a respected headmaster, still bears the scars of a school timetable which as a secondary school boy subjected him for a whole year to one morning a week of Latin, followed by French, followed by Latin again, followed by mathematics. Probably similar scars are carried by the poor mathematics teacher, who was forced to take the last lesson in this somewhat indigestible line-up. Whether there was some special reason for this timetabling howler or whether no one noticed it until it was too late, there is little doubt that the class and the teachers concerned are hardly likely to have given of their best under the circumstances.

Lesson planning. Turning from the general timetable to the timetable within lessons themselves (i.e., to the way in which activities are planned within each lesson), something of the same considerations remains. Not only should each lesson, as far as possible, be planned so that the transitions from one activity to another are smooth and not too frequent, care should be taken to see that these transitions introduce appropriate and welcome variety. An over-lengthy period of teacher talk, for example, followed by a period of hectic practical activity, is likely to invite a degree of mayhem during the latter. Similarly a lesson which contains nothing but teacher talk is likely to invite its own brand of disruption from the children.

Even in the best planned and organized lesson, particular attention should be given to the mechanics of how the move from one activity to another is to take place. Such movement, together with the periods at the beginning and the end of the lesson, are always potentially difficult times, when the teacher's ability to guide and administer what is going on is under particular strain. Here the successful teacher is the one who makes it clear to children in advance what is expected of them during the time concerned, and who is therefore able to monitor carefully what is going on and draw attention immediately to any deviations from the laid-down instructions.

Class organization. Turning to class organization and administration, it is clear that at all ages class control problems can be created by a simple failure to provide children with the right conditions in which to work. Cramped classrooms, in which there is insufficient space for children to carry out practical activities, and open-plan units where the noise from other groups becomes intrusive are obvious examples. So are seating arrangements which prevent all children from easily seeing the work being presented or demonstrated by the teacher, or classrooms which have obvious distractions (e.g., the games fields) just outside the window. But even where facilities are ideal, the teacher can often cause problems for him or herself simply by failing to ensure that all necessary equipment is readily to hand, that the activities going on in one part of the room do not conflict with those being carried out in an adjacent part, and that children are aware of a few simple, sensible rules designed to make everyone's work easier. This is particularly important in infant and junior school classrooms, where the level of classroom circulation and of practical pastimes is likely to be high, but it is also crucial to secondary schools where experimental or technical or creative work is underway (e.g., science, craft, physical education, drama and art lessons).

Teacher personality and classroom atmosphere. It is also relevant to point out that, just as there are variations in preferred working environment between children (see the discussion of affective factors in Chapter 2) so teachers also differ in the kind of surroundings in which they function best. An extraverted teacher may well be quite at home in a noisy, bustling environment, whereas an introverted teacher might well prefer a quieter and more settled context. A confident, experienced teacher might be quite at home with the knowledge that colleagues can see him or her at work, while a more retiring or less experienced person might prefer to be able to shut the classroom door and carry on with the class in private. Some teachers rather welcome the endless series of interruptions by small message-bearers that go on in the primary school, while others find themselves driven to near distraction.

Unfortunately, very little account is taken by local education authorities, school designers, and even sometimes by headteachers of individual teacher's likes and dislikes. An introverted teacher in a school full of bouncy extraverted colleagues will often end up feeling inadequate because of his or her need for quiet working conditions, while an extravert in a school staffed mainly by introverts will often come to feel noisy and gauche and a constant irritation to colleagues. A teacher who dislikes working in an open-plan school may feel old-fashioned and the odd one out in a school which operates open-plan successfully, while an open-plan supporter may feel worryingly isolated from colleagues and other children while operating in a conventional building where each teacher functions behind a closed classroom door.

What I am saying is that one teacher may find it difficult to maintain what he or she considers to be good class control in a certain working environment, while another teacher may find that this environment brings out the best in them in terms of professional skills whereas another working environment is less suitable. But there is even more to it than this. Teachers operating in what is for them an unsuitable building or unsuitable classroom may find that the strain upon the nerves tends to make them irritable with the children, causing the children to become resentful in their own turn and to be less co-operative with whatever the teacher is trying to do. Thus in addition to the sheer problems caused by the working environment, there are deteriorations in teacher–child relationships as well. Small wonder that problems of class control emerge in such situations, or that teachers find their work particularly stressful (a point I return to in Chapter 8).

A similar strain can of course be placed upon the teacher by another variable, often closely related to matters of school organization and planning, namely the school's educational philosophy. If the school is run on so-called 'informal' lines, the teacher who holds what might be described as a more subject-centred or structured approach to learning might well become unhappy and disoriented with a class of children who he or she feels are deliberately being invited by the school to flout the standards and working practices which he or she considers important. A more informal teacher in a more formal school, however, might well find that it is the children who are becoming unhappy and disoriented since they are being offered one standard of behaviour by him or her yet are being penalized for operating that standard with other teachers. Either way, the resulting problems in terms of class control are obvious. So indeed are the problems which occur for any teacher who takes a class for a lesson immediately after they have been taught by a particularly strict colleague. Far from being still subdued, the children are likely to allow their feelings of pent-up energy to be given very positive expression as they move into a more permissive environment, thus causing control problems which are neither of the children's nor of the teacher's making.

The probationary teacher and control problems

For the student or for the probationary teacher, there are likely to be particular problems associated simply with lack of experience. In the case of the student, things are made harder by the children's recognition of the fact that the student does not carry the status or authority of a full member of staff. Not surprisingly, a degree of limit testing of the kind described in Chapter 2 is likely to take place, and if the student reacts to this with obvious signs of dismay on the one hand, or aggression on the other, things are likely to get worse. By rising, in a sense, to the children's bait, the student is indicating the power that the class has to discomfort him or her personally and unsettle his or her attempts at teaching them. The nearness of age between the student or probationary teacher and the class, though it carries with it certain advantages, is from the class control point of view also likely to be something of a handicap.

An even greater handicap may be the young teacher's lack of knowledge of accepted standards, practices, rituals and traditions within the school, a lack of knowledge which the children will naturally enough be tempted to exploit whenever possible. Another temptation is the teacher's lack of knowledge of what work the class has already covered with previous teachers. Here there are endless opportunities for debate and disagreement amongst the children whenever the question of whether a particular topic has or has not been covered arises. While the teacher vainly tries to keep order, the children throw claims and counter-claims at each other, often taking the opportunity, through heaped scorn and insults, to prosecute running inter-classroom feuds or to express their contempt for their last teacher. But however intense the in-fighting, it is often the teacher who is really the butt of the class, being ridiculed in a sense for not knowing things which are perfectly familiar to the children themselves, and being as a consequence made to feel very much the outsider.

Lack of knowledge of the community in which the school is situated, and therefore of the children's backgrounds, is another major handicap; as is the new teacher's lack of knowledge of the children's individual academic performance and even of such basic essentials as their names. He or she may also not be familiar with the schemes of work operating within the school, nor with the textbooks from which the children are studying, nor with the friendship and rivalry patterns within the class. All these are practical matters which are discussed further in Part II, but again for present purposes the point simply is that it is factors within the teacher which are leading to the control problems. The longer the teacher takes before these factors are corrected, and the more he or she shows in the meanwhile that the children are disturbing him or her, the worse these problems are likely to become.

Far better for the student or teacher to start learning everything possible about the children and the school as quickly as possible, maintaining at the same time an equanimity compounded as necessary of firm decisive action and calm resolve in the face of the children's assaults upon his or her composure.

References

Michael Rutter's work can be sampled in: Rutter, M. (1975) *Helping Troubled Children*. Harmondsworth: Penguin.

For the incidence and influence of educational failure see: Fontana, D. (1984) Failures of academic achievement. In: A. Gale and A.J. Chapman (eds) *Psychology and Social Problems*. Chichester: Wiley.

Part 2. Guiding and Reshaping Problem Behaviours

Chapter 4

Strategies I:
The Behavioural Approach

In Chapter 2 I discussed the idea that many behaviour problems are in fact learnt attention-seeking strategies. The child learns through what is sometimes termed *operant conditioning* (or trial and error learning) that certain forms of behaviour appear to win the attention which is being sought, and in consequence these forms of behaviour become part of his or her established repertoire. I also discussed the point that since many teachers are unaware of what is going on, they frequently inadvertently reinforce in the child the very behaviours that as teachers they most wish to discourage. For example, they may reward children with attention every time they misbehave, and ignore them when they are co-operating. The fact that this attention is angry or disapproving attention may be unimportant. The point is that the child is succeeding in distracting the teacher from class-work, and is in consequence often allowed to feel a significant and indeed even powerful member of the class.

This applies, of course, only to disruptive pupils. The majority of children are able to gain the teacher's attention by producing acceptable behaviours, and may be strongly motivated to avoid doing anything likely to invoke disapproval. But for those children who have been brought up in the kind of conditions described in Chapter 2, the whole process of learning how to behave in conformity with the general standards and practices of the school is a much more difficult task, and the teacher can only understand the child's behaviour if this difficulty is taken into account.

Over the last two decades, and particularly since 1970, an attempt to systematize some of the major practical issues associated with this difficulty has been made in the USA and in the UK. Known variously as the *behavioural approach* to classroom management or as *behaviour modification* this approach has demonstrated that by introducing *precision* into the business of teacher–child relationships much can be done to improve the behaviour of even the most troublesome children. Behaviour modification takes its starting point from the recognition that behaviour which is rewarded tends to be repeated, while behaviour that receives no rewards tends to be eliminated. Thus many of our actions can only be understood if we examine the rewards or consequences that follow upon these actions (see Chapter 2). Based upon the work of the American psychologist Fred Skinner, behaviour modification suggests, therefore, that in the classroom we must always look closely at the way the teacher or the rest of the class respond to what a particular child does if we are to recognize why he or she continues to do it.

The behaviour modification approach, then, insists that if we want to change the child's behaviour we must first change the way in which in the past we have tended to respond to this behaviour. To take the main example of attention-seeking behaviour, this means that if we have been rewarding 'bad' behaviour with attention (angry or otherwise), and ignoring for the most part 'good' behaviour, then we must reverse our response processes and start ignoring the bad behaviour as much as possible and rewarding the good. This sounds simple enough, but of course it raises all kinds of questions and potential problems, and we need to try and deal with these by embarking upon a rather fuller explanation of what is actually involved.

The behavioural approach to classroom problems

The theory behind the behavioural approach is as follows:

1. *Observable behaviour can be described in objective terms.* The main concern of the psychologist, and of the teacher as an applied psychologist, is with *observable behaviour*. We may enjoy speculating about motives and about the 'reasons' why people decide to act as they do, but all this is somewhat imprecise since we cannot actually see these motives and these reasons. We have to rely upon what people tell us about them, and people may be genuinely unaware of what their real motives are, or may choose deliberately to mislead us about them. Behaviour, on the other hand, is something objectively observable and something about which any group of reliable witnesses can usefully agree.

2. *Behaviour is learnt. The majority of human behaviours are learnt.*

Thus if these behaviours are unacceptable for some reason, we can help the person producing them to unlearn them and to learn something more appropriate in their place.

3. *The law of effect.* Learning is based primarily upon the process of operant conditioning (trial and error). Operant conditioning obeys the law of effect, which in the simple wording used above means that behaviour which is rewarded tends to be repeated, while behaviour that receives no reward tends to be eliminated.

4. *Change the contingencies.* If we wish to help someone unlearn unwanted behaviours and learn something more appropriate in their place, therefore, we must change the way in which that someone is rewarded or not rewarded for his or her actions.

The context of learning. In addition, behaviourism insists that we should take into account the context in which behaviour occurs. Thus we must not assume that simply because the child learns that one form of behaviour is successful in obtaining desired rewards in Mr Green's classroom he or she will necessarily automatically produce it in Mrs White's. The child may have found early on through trial and error that what works with Mr Green stands very little chance with Mrs White, and in consequence he or she will have learnt a different set of strategies for relating to the latter.

Implications for the teacher. What does this behavioural theory mean in terms of the teacher's practical concerns? It means essentially that he or she must take into account the child's *behaviour*, the *consequences* of that behaviour, and the *context* in which that behaviour occurs. By studying these three variables, the teacher is enabled to understand much more clearly what is actually happening when misbehaviour occurs, and what strategies should be adopted to discourage this misbehaviour and to encourage something more desirable in its place. Let us look in detail at how he or she goes about this.

Recording the observations: deficits

The first step is to sit down, preferably in the relaxed atmosphere of your own home where objective thinking about what happens in the classroom is more possible, and make a careful list of the behaviours in a particular child that are giving cause for concern. Here it must be stressed that these behaviours must be listed *in detail*. It is of no value simply to write down something like 'disruptive', or 'hostile'.

We need to know the precise behaviours that go to make up this disruption and this hostility. Does the child:

- come into the classroom noisily?
- come in consistently late?
- slouch to his or her place with every sign of reluctance?
- engage in by-play with other children and if so of what does the by-play consist?
- fail to produce a text book when asked?
- call out in class?
- make insulting remarks to the teacher or to other children, and if so what form do these remarks usually take?
- physically threaten other children, and if so how?

The simple act of breaking the child's difficult behaviour down into its component elements gives the teacher the feeling that a start has been made. The child has been shown to be 'analysable'. What seemed hitherto like a concertedly disruptive front can now be seen in fact to consist of a collection of separate behaviours, each one of them potentially capable of solution. Having drawn up the list, and allowed him or herself to feel a little better about things as a consequence, the next step for the teacher is to write down against each of the child's unwanted behaviours the usual response to that behaviour which the teacher offers, e.g.

Child behaviour	*Teacher response*
Noisy entry into classroom	'How many times have I told you to come in quietly?'
Calls out loudly to friend	'Get out and come in again without that performance'
Comes in again smirking	'And take that grin off your face'
Sits down but fails to get books out when asked	'I suppose it would be too much to expect you to take any interest in what we're doing'
Turns round and engages in noisy conversation with neighbours	'Come and sit in this desk at the front'
Sits at the front and proceeds to pull faces at classmates	Touches child and turns his or her head around to face the front

If the list is a long one there is no need to put down the exact remarks made by the teacher, since these will vary from lesson to lesson just as will certain of the child's specific activities. But the list will contain precise specifications of each of the child's aggravating activities, and against each one of these must be entered the teacher's usual kind of response.

Once the list has been drawn up, the teacher can study it to see what kind of pattern appears to emerge. All too often, as in the case of the above example, it will become clear that what is happening is that the teacher is responding to the bait which the child is offering. The latter is coming in late or noisily because it is obvious that this gets him or her noticed by the teacher and makes the teacher behave in an unsettled way. The child is succeeding in annoying the teacher. Although the behaviourist does not choose to speculate on how this makes the child feel, since 'feeling' in this context is not an observable part of behaviour, we can nevertheless add that success in annoying the teacher probably gives the child a sense of personal significance and power. And if it also attracts the attention of the rest of the class, so much the better.

Recording the observations: the good points

Having drawn up the first list, the job of the teacher is now to draw up a second one which records instances of the child's wanted behaviours and of his or her response to them on the odd occasions when they do happen to occur. Often this list will be almost the exact opposite of the first one. Instead of writing 'noisy entry into classroom' the teacher will write 'quiet entry into classroom', and instead of writing 'calls out loudly to friend across room' writes 'takes place in classroom quietly'.

When it comes to recording the teacher response to these behaviours, however, the teacher will often find that there is a somewhat surprising blank. On those rare times when the child does as he or she is told the teacher seems to offer nothing in the way of a response. There is no attention directed at the child, and therefore no reward. Is it any wonder that these wanted behaviours tend to occur only infrequently? Their lack of success in attracting teacher attention ensures that they do not become an established part of the child's behavioural repertoire.

Looking at the two lists together, the teacher can then see that without realizing it he or she has been rewarding the undesirable behaviour and failing to reward the desirable. Moreover, the teacher can see that those behaviours which were intended at the time to be punitive (i.e., speaking sharply to the child, drawing attention to misdemeanours) were in fact nothing of the kind. From the child's point of view they were a form of reward, and therefore served to ensure the repetition of the behaviour concerned.

Identif ing reinforcers and examining teacher behaviours

Once t e teacher has drawn up the lists, it will be possible to see that reinforcers come in a variety of forms. I have already discussed the most important one, and the one that is most directly under the teacher's control, namely teacher attention. But the response of the rest of the class is obviously important. If a child finds that a particular action tends to amuse the rest of the class and dispose them favourably towards him or her, then it is likely to be repeated whenever the opportunity (the *context*, to use the term which has been already introduced) presents itself. Or it may be that the child's actions appeal to a close group of friends, or to a member of the opposite sex whom he or she is trying to impress. Or perhaps the actions get the child out of doing something that is disliked, as, for example, when he or she proves apparently incapable of giving a sensible response to difficult class questions and the teacher gives up directing them towards him or her. Or it may be that the child's apparent inability to look after school property persuades the teacher to stop insisting he or she take school textbooks home and complete homework like the rest of the class, or to stay on after school and help with some rather tedious set of chores.

Punishments and rewards: intended and unintended. Drawing up the lists as described has another advantage, however, in that it helps the teacher examine more closely the influence of punishment upon child behaviour. Just as behaviour that is reinforced tends to recur, so behaviour that is punished tends to be discontinued. And whether we like the idea or not, a great deal of what the teacher takes to be 'punishment' does in fact get offered to children during the course of most lessons. The teacher will verbally reprimand, will deduct house points, will mark work wrong, will move children to sit at the front, will send children out of the room or to visit the headteacher, will set impositions, will curtail privileges, and will impose a range of sanctions involving such things as the whole class working in silence or the abrupt termination of an enjoyable class-room task and its replacement with one that is much less popular. The assumption on the part of the teacher each time the punishment is imposed is that it will curtail unwanted behaviour and encourage something more acceptable in its place.

As has already been demonstrated, however, not all punishments are what they appear to be. The teacher assumes that by speaking sharply to a child the child is being punished, whereas the child may experience such action as a direct form of reward. When we look at our list, therefore, we may realize that what we construed as punishment was received by the child in fact in a quite different light. Similarly, stopping a child's games or keeping him or her in during playtime or break may seem like punishment from the teacher's point of view, but from the point of view of the child may seem like a welcome break from an activity which is not enjoyed, or from going out in the cold. Or it may be that punishment carries with it increased status for the child concerned, as it allows him or her to demonstrate bravado in front of the rest of the class. Or it may allow the child to feel contemptuous of the teacher, since the punishment is obviously taken so seriously by the teacher yet bothers the child not in the least. Or it could be that the punishment is regarded as a great joke since it is invariably accompanied by an entertaining display of rage on the teacher's part.

Conversely, and more constructively, many things that perhaps appeared not to be in the least punitive can be seen as quite potent in their actual effects. Ignoring a child is one such thing, and one which is likely to be readily apparent once the list is carefully studied. Another might have to do with the casual remark made to a parent at a parent's evening, or the comment put upon an end-of-term report. Another might relate to the teacher's refusal to let the class see a television programme or to use a coveted piece of apparatus. True, many of these items may not show up directly on the list, since they relate to incidents which may occur outside the lesson, but references to them almost certainly will. Thus the teacher may mention to a child in passing that he or she must remember to tell the child's parents of a particular piece of misbehaviour at the next opportunity, or suggest that owing to the problems the child has been causing there won't be time for the class to see the television programme or to use the new piece of equipment. None of these may be intended as direct threats; nevertheless the teacher may be able to see when perusing the list that for the remainder of that lesson at least the child's behaviour was markedly improved.

This must not be taken to mean that I am encouraging the use of punishment and threats as a way of securing and maintaining classroom control. Threats and punishments have drawbacks of their own, and I discuss these later in the chapter. But teachers do use minor punishments and sanctions as a routine part of their work and if these punishments and sanctions are to be effective then the teacher must take the opportunity of examining carefully the observable effects that they seem to have upon children's behaviour. Without such examination, teachers will not only inadvertently be offering rewards when they imagine they are offering punishments, but will also fail to see the potential punitive impact that certain actions available to them might actually have.

Modifying unwanted behaviours

Let us suppose that the teacher has now drawn up the suggested lists for an individual child who is causing problems in the classroom. The child's behaviour has been recorded together with the teacher's responses to that behaviour. How does the teacher now proceed? The next step is to record the *context* in which the child's unwanted behaviour occurs, and then to keep a record over a few days of certain selected items of that behaviour in order to obtain a note of its *frequency*.

The context. Taking context first, the teacher may find that the unwanted behaviour only occurs when other children (or when certain other children) are also present. Or maybe it only occurs in language lessons and not in literature, or on Monday mornings but not on Fridays, or when the teacher has been taking the whole class to task over some matter, or when reprimanding the child for not bringing in homework. By noting the context, the teacher will become aware of the set of circumstances which appear to trigger off the undesirable behaviour in the child. Sometimes this in itself is sufficient evidence for him or her to know how to behave in future. If the child tends to play up only when reprimanded in front of the rest of the class, then care should be taken as far as possible to issue reprimands in private or out of earshot of the class. If the child reacts badly on a Monday but not on a Friday (sometimes evidence of a disturbed home, with the child at his or her worst after being with the family over the weekend), then more interesting work can perhaps be scheduled for the Monday in the hope of keeping him or her more happily occupied. Or if the child is particularly difficult after coming from say a physical education lesson, then a word with the teacher concerned to try and clarify some of the factors which stimulate this difficult behaviour would be in order.

The frequency of undesirable behaviour. As far as keeping a record of frequency is concerned, the object is to identify just how persistent a particular problem actually is, and to provide baseline data against which can be charted any improvement after a behaviour modification programme has been got under way. This record can take the form of simply placing a mark upon a piece of paper each time the unwanted behaviour occurs, and then adding up these marks at the end of the lesson. If the behaviour is particularly frequent, it can be recorded for the first five minutes in every half hour, or for any other short interval that the teacher feels able easily to handle. But whatever the system adopted, neither the child nor the rest of the class should be aware of what is going on. If the child is producing a range of unwanted behaviours, then it may be impractical to record more than a limited number of them at any one time, and the teacher should therefore concentrate initially only upon those behaviours to be tackled immediately.

As to which these behaviours actually are it must be left to the individual teacher to decide. One strategy is to list the behaviours in order of their apparent amenability to the particular behavioural approach that the teacher is planning to adopt. Suppose this approach is simply to withhold reinforcement from unwanted behaviours by ignoring them (the simplest and most widely used approach). The list might then range from 'entering classroom noisily' (most easily ignored) to 'punching other children' (least easily ignored). The teacher might as a result decide to employ ignoring behaviour towards 'entering classroom noisily' and perhaps towards the next two or three items on the list, while for the moment carrying on as normal towards all the others. This will provide an opportunity to test out the effectiveness of the behavioural approach towards the child concerned, while at the same time not interfering with any of the strategies that are being used towards behaviours which appear to demand some more direct form of intervention.

Of course, it may well be that these latter behaviours are not susceptible to treatment by ignoring at any time, and I look at alternative ways of responding to them shortly. But sticking for a moment to simple behaviours that seem to fall into this category, what does the teacher now do? To take the first item on the list, 'entering the classroom noisily', the teacher now refuses to respond in any way when the child makes a loud arrival. The teacher neither speaks to him or her nor even bothers to glance in their direction. Instead he or she carries on calmly with what is being done, whether it be talking to another child or getting out books, and gives no indication that anything untoward has been noticed. Each time the child enters noisily, he or she receives the same reception. Thus each noisy entry receives no reinforcement from the teacher, with the result that, in an ideal world, this noisy behaviour gradually becomes 'extinguished' (to use the technical term), and the child has learnt to come in quietly.

Unfortunately, the classroom is far from an ideal world, and it may well be that the child will become noisier and noisier in attempts to capture the teacher's attention until there comes a point when ignoring becomes very difficult indeed, particularly if other members of the class take it into their heads to start following this example. If the teacher decides to persevere with the ignoring behaviour come what may, then after reaching a crescendo the noisy entry will begin to tail off, but the process may take a long time and the strain on the teacher's nerves may make the whole business hardly worthwhile. So 'ignoring' on its own is rarely enough. It must be combined with another strategy if it is going to become a realistic proposition for the great majority of teachers.

This other strategy is not far to seek. If we think back to the original description of how to draw up a list of the child's behaviours it will be remembered that there were in fact two lists rather than only one. The second list consisted of those *desirable* behaviours that were to be encouraged at the same time that the undesirable ones were being discouraged. Teachers must therefore not restrict themselves simply to ignoring the unwanted behaviour, they must actively find opportunities to encourage the wanted behaviour. This is called by some psychologists 'catching the child being good'. The teacher must catch the child being good, and see to it that he or she is rewarded with teacher attention, or with whatever other reinforcement is being used, each time this happens.

And I really mean *each time it happens*. In the early stages, reinforcement is very much more effective if it is applied without fail each time the wanted behaviour is produced. This may seem a counsel of perfection, but as Chapter 5 shows, it is a characteristic of effective teachers that they have a very good idea of what is going on in the classroom at all times throughout the lesson. Indeed the problem may be not so much having to catch the disruptive child being good so frequently, but to hunt for any occasions when he or she is being good at all. The child may seem to produce the wanted behaviours so rarely, that however hard the teacher tries it may be almost impossible to have any opportunity of reinforcing from one end of the lesson to the other.

Shaping. At this point I have to introduce another concept used in the behavioural approach to classroom control, namely that of *shaping*. Briefly, the notion of shaping is that although the child may not produce the behaviour we actually want, nevertheless he or she will produce from time to time behaviour that approximates to it, or that at least resembles it more closely than does his or her normal behaviour. Thus to return to the example of noisy classroom entry behaviour, it may be that although the child never comes in quietly there are nevertheless occasions when he or she comes in less noisily than usual. By responding to the child on these occasions, the behavioural approach suggests, the teacher will find that it is gradually possible to shape behaviour in the desired direction. The incidence of quieter entrances will increase, while the incidence of noisier ones will decrease, until a point will be reached where the teacher has to be careful not to miss the child's entry altogether.

In practical terms, what this means is that the teacher will look up and smile at the child and offer a pleasant remark when he or she comes in relatively quietly, while still ignoring the child when the entry is noisy. At first the child may be taken somewhat aback. He or she will hardly be used to being greeted with a smile by a teacher, still less with a welcoming remark. But after the first few occasions this welcoming attention will be found to be much pleasanter, and therefore more reinforcing than disapproving attention, and certainly much more pleasant than being ignored. So the quiet entry will become routine and – of great importance – the friendlier footing upon which teacher and child start the lesson may exert a beneficial influence on the latter's subsequent behaviour.

I must stress that the 'welcoming remark' to which I refer in the above paragraph need not take the form of congratulating the child on coming in quietly. In fact it is better if it does not. To offer congratulation in this way only indicates to the child that the teacher has in fact been noticing the usual noisy arrival, even though affecting to ignore it. The impact of this ignoring will therefore be lessened in future. Far better simply to make some incidental remark to the child, of the kind that the teacher will be offering to many of the other children as a matter of course. The teacher may say for example that he or she has heard the child was running a local disco at the weekend, or played well for a local football team, or took part in a sponsored walk. Or the teacher may ask a direct and interested question about one of the child's activities. If the interchange between teacher and child is overheard by the rest of the class and draws attention to something in which the child has been successful, then so much the better. The teacher will now be offering prestige in the eyes of the other children, which will greatly increase the reinforcing effect of the attention.

Once a particular piece of desirable behaviour has become firmly established, it is no longer necessary to seek to reinforce it each time it happens. Indeed to do so can become counter-productive, in that the child becomes so habituated to teacher attention and praise that it no longer carries particular value. Reinforcement from time to time becomes sufficient, in particular when this reinforcement is offered primarily for particularly good examples of the behaviour concerned.

Having worked successfully on some of the simpler aspects of the child's behaviour, the teacher is now ready to try the behavioural approach in other areas. As already indicated, an advantage when moving on to these other areas is that the very fact of having established a pleasanter relationship with the child on such things as classroom entry behaviour will have a beneficial influence upon more demanding work. The child will now have come to associate the teacher with a more friendly and relaxed response, and in consequence will be more favourably disposed towards further attempts to guide him or her in appropriate directions. The teacher may now try 'catching the child being good' or shaping the child towards 'being good' at such things as staying seated instead of getting up and walking around whenever the urge arises, at putting up a hand and waiting quietly to be asked, at working individually instead of interfering with other children, at speaking sociably to the teacher instead of being rude and hostile.

As these behaviours are dealt with one by one, the teacher will often be pleasantly surprised to see that other undesirable behaviours begin to disappear apparently of their own accord. As the child begins to enjoy a more friendly relationship with the teacher, and begins to learn that attention and prestige can be gained by producing acceptable behaviours, so will many of the anti-social strategies become increasingly unnecessary, and will disappear from the repertoire to be replaced by other more appropriate ones without the teacher having to tackle them directly.

One essential word of caution is necessary here. The teacher must be careful not to allow concern with academic work *per se* to interfere with the operation of the strategies we have been discussing. It is of little value to greet children pleasantly when they come into the room, and then to spend the whole lesson berating them for the low standard of written work. Nor is it of much use to invite a child to provide the answer to a class question as a reward for waiting quietly with a hand up only to tell the child in no uncertain fashion that the answer is wrong. In these and in other similar instances the methods that the teacher is using to reshape the child's social behaviours must also be directed towards academic work. Shaping is particularly important here, with the child being praised and encouraged for work which approximates, albeit initially very slightly, towards the desired standards. So is the ability to separate in the teacher's own mind the child's desirable behaviour from the undesirable. Thus, for example, if a child is waiting quietly with a hand up to answer a class question, this in itself is desirable, irrespective of whether the answer itself is correct or not (i.e., desirable or undesirable). In consequence the teacher will see to it that not only is the child rewarded by being asked to provide the answer, but that this answer is treated seriously and with respect even if it is wrong. The teacher can indicate this by smiling and thanking the child for a good attempt, or by giving reassurance that the mistake is a perfectly understandable one, or (if appropriate) by giving praise for being on the right lines.

Provided the teacher's response is friendly and encouraging in this way, the child will feel reinforced by it and will be prompted to employ the same quiet 'hand up' behaviour in the future. On the other hand if the child is told abruptly that the answer is wrong, or worse still that it is thoughtless and silly, the humiliation of this experience in front of the rest of the class will be sufficient to discourage the child from attempting the 'hand up' behaviour next time. After all, why demonstrate to the class that you are trying your best if it is obvious that your best is not good enough? Why put your prestige and status at stake only to be shown by the teacher how sadly you are lacking? Far better to confine yourself to calling out deliberately silly answers in order to amuse and impress your friends. And that way you can always pretend to all and sundry (including yourself) that you could easily get the answers right if school were actually worth the effort.

Rewards and punishments

Having looked in some detail at the behavioural approach to

managing unwanted behaviours in individual children, something needs to be said about rewards and punishments before moving on any further.

A simple definition of a reward is that it is something (material or non-material) that appears desirable to the person concerned. Punishment, by contrast, is something that appears positively undesirable. The stronger the feeling of desire attached towards a particular thing, the greater its potential power as a reward. Conversely the stronger the feelings of aversion towards something, the greater its potential power as a punishment. Operant conditioning, on which the behavioural approach is based, claims that where actions are followed by reward they tend to become established, and where actions are followed by no reward or by punishment they tend to disappear. In theory, the stronger the reward the more likely is it that the behaviour will become established, and the stronger the punishment the more likely is it that the behaviour will disappear.

In practice, it does not work out quite like this. A reward may, for example, prove so desirable when gained the first time that we may be over-anxious when we try for it on a second occasion, with the result that our behaviour second time around may not be so effective as it was first time. Similarly a punishment may be so alarming first time that, paralysed by fear, we become confused and find ourselves repeating our mistake and being punished yet again on the second occasion. An obvious example at school level in terms of reward would be the child who gives a faultless performance first time at some task and is so overcome by public praise that he or she makes a mess of it next time. An equally obvious example in terms of punishment would be the child who makes a series of stumbling errors in front of the class and is so laughed at and ridiculed that he or she does exactly the same thing when commanded by the teacher to try again.

What is a reward? However, while keeping these important exceptions in mind, it is fair to say that if we can find appropriate rewards to offer to children it will make our chances of shaping their behaviour that much easier. Similarly if we can find appropriate punishments. But what do we mean by appropriate? This is the crucial question. The school and the teacher only have in fact a very limited range of such gifts and sanctions available to them. And in any case we all feel that the ideal is to work at something 'for its own sake' rather than for any external reward, while at the same time we baulk at the whole notion of punishment in a civilized and caring adult–child relationship.

But if we look at the matter objectively, we see that many of the most important rewards in life consist of relatively common things (human warmth, friendly gestures, social acceptance, encouragement, the good opinion of others), while many of the most effective punishments consist simply of the absence or withholding of these things. Similarly we also see that the notions of doing things 'for their own sake' or of avoiding all punishments are for the most part illusory. If we read a poem for the delight of poetry, for example, we are not doing it for the poem's own 'sake'. The poem, presumably, has no awareness of the fact that we are reading it. We read it for the pleasure it gives us, for our own 'sake', for the reward offered to us by our feelings of pleasure. And if we give children a frown of disapproval for some inappropriate action we are punishing them whether we like it or not by signalling to them the withdrawal of our approval. So daily life consists of rewards and punishments, no matter how small, much of the time. And these rewards and punishments play a large part in moulding and directing our behaviour.

Let us therefore discard the idea that by 'rewards' we are discussing glittering prizes, or that by 'punishments' we are discussing something harsh and painful. We are simply helping children to see that certain behaviours produce desirable consequences in a responsible, aware society, while other forms of behaviour do not. As children grow older, so they will become more and more able to see such things for themselves, and will be able to take responsibility for their own behaviour.

Having accepted rewards and punishments (though sanctions is on balance a less fearsome word than 'punishment') as part of the normal learning process, is there anything further that can be said about the effectiveness of the particular strategies which they include? Certainly there is, and we can begin by taking a closer look at rewards.

Types of classroom rewards

From the behavioural perspective, rewards are thought of primarily in terms of objective reinforcers supplied by the external environment. In consequence, the behavioural approach to classroom control says little about the subjective, internal rewards that come from the individual's own sense of self-satisfaction. It is not that the latter are dismissed as unimportant, simply that they are not under the direct influence of the teacher in the way that external rewards are. I look closely at these internal rewards in the next chapter, when I turn from the behavioural approach to what is known as the *cognitive* approach, but for the moment I am concerned with rewards of the external kind. These can be roughly divided into two groups:

1. *Non-material rewards.* These consist primarily of such things as teacher attention, teacher praise, teacher encouragement, peer-group attention (primarily of the positive, friendly kind), and attention and praise from agencies outside the immediate classroom, such as year tutors, headteachers, and the whole school.

2. *Material rewards.* These are made up of good marks, good termly reports, house points and stars, privileges, special responsibilities, badges of office and other such tokens.

Obviously the two groups are closely linked, in that material rewards are of value chiefly because they stand as tangible marks of teacher attention and esteem, while non-material rewards are often of benefit because they hold the promise of something more tangible in the future, such as privileges or entry into a chosen occupation on leaving school. But from the point of view of class control, it is convenient to think of them separately.

Non material rewards. These are the very stuff of classroom control. The successful teacher is constantly drawing the attention of children to standards and achievements within their own individual work, and praising and encouraging them as a consequence. This praise and encouragement has a vital role to play in keeping children involved and interested in their work, and in helping them to build upon current achievements by raising their confidence and their belief in their own abilities. To have maximum effect, behavioural research shows that such praise and encouragement should follow as *immediately* as possible upon the child's perform-ance of the good work concerned. Thus the teacher who is con-tinually monitoring children and is quick to draw attention to success is likely to be using praise and encouragement more effectively than is the teacher who only hands out favourable comments when, for example, marked written work is being returned. And both teachers are likely to be more effective than the teacher who rarely if ever praises the great majority of children, and only utters a few grudging words to the very ablest children on the rarest of occasions.

Clearly, of course, all praise and encouragement should be linked to some observable standards. If they are handed out indiscriminately they soon lose their force. But these standards should be as far as possible individual things, linked to the possibilities open to each child at that particular time. Thus in both individual and in class work, the succesful teacher is the one who is swift to identify and reward anything which indicates appropriate effort on the part of the child concerned, irrespective of how this work compares with what is being produced by the rest of the class. If the teacher does this without appearing condescending on the one hand or artificially lavish on the other, the class will quickly come to understand that it is not a case of operating multiple standards. The teacher is simply, in an objective and matter of fact way, awarding praise where praise is due. Such praise is therefore seen as *realistic* praise.

In addition to being realistic, praise and encouragement should also be *consistent* if they are to be of maximum value. It is of no value to praise a particular action one day and to praise its exact opposite the next. Or to praise children for something one day and punish them for it (for example by deliberately and obviously ignoring them) the next. Such inconsistency leads to confused behaviour in children. The class needs to be aware of the standards and procedures which operate in the classroom, and to be clear that the production of certain kinds of behaviour will lead consistently to certain kinds of desired rewards. For example, hard work is always encouraged, irrespective of the level of attainment of the child concerned. Creativity is encouraged, even if its results may be somewhat bizarre at times. Thoughtfulness towards others is praised. Waiting one's turn is rewarded by the desired attention. Honesty is praised, even if the confession of a misdemeanour may carry inevitably certain sanctions for the child concerned. Politeness and respect are met with politeness and respect.

Finally, the effectiveness of non-material rewards depends closely upon the *prestige and status* in which the person giving the rewards is held. If a teacher is admired and liked by the class, then generally individuals will value his or her praise and encouragement. Such praise and encouragement will indicate to the child that progress is being made in a desirable direction, and will also increase, importantly, his or her standing with the rest of the class. An additional benefit, of course, is that it further enhances the relationship between the teacher and the child, and renders the latter more likely to produce behaviour leading to further teacher rewards in the future. As to the important question of what gives a teacher prestige and status in the eyes of individual children and the class, I have more to say in Chapters 5 and 7.

Non-material rewards, therefore, are at their most effective when they are:

- as *immediate* as possible
- *realistic*
- applied *consistently*
- awarded by a person who carries *prestige and status* in the eyes of the recipient.

Material rewards. The same is also true of material rewards, though these usually carry some desirable intrinsic value too, as with certain privileges. They can in addition, particularly in the case of good termly reports, attract further rewards outside the school, notably parental approval and perhaps in consequence yet more privileges and treats. Thus the awarding or withholding of material rewards in school can be an effective aid to the teacher in the maintenance of classroom control, and certainly should never be treated in the somewhat dismissive fashion that obtains on occasions when it comes, for example, to the writing of termly or yearly reports.

The token economy. Much has been written in recent years about the way in which the giving and witholding of material rewards can be built into a complete system for the maintenance of control and the modification of behaviour. Under this system, sometimes known as the *token economy*, children are awarded points or tokens each time they produce a previously agreed item of behaviour (staying seated for periods of five minutes at a time in class perhaps, or refraining from aggressive behaviour towards others during a lesson, or handing in work on time, or virtually any other identifiable target behaviour). At the end of a given period, which may be each day initially and then each week or longer, the tokens can be exchanged at an agreed rate for a special privilege.

Such token economies work best in closed institutions, such as residential schools, where the reward system is under the extensive control of those in authority and where the children's behaviour can be monitored throughout the day. They are less likely to be effective in an open community like the ordinary school, where the staff have contact with the children for only a limited time, and where staff–pupil ratios are not favourable enough to allow the close and continuous monitoring of individual children's behaviour which the token economy ideally demands. Nevertheless, in a modified form the token economy does have a place in the ordinary school in certain circumstances, provided that the staff are all agreed as to its value, know what is involved, and operate it consistently.

The performance contract. One example of this is in the use of what is called a performance contract. The simplest example of the performance contract is the report card. The child is put 'on report' by the headteacher, and has each lesson to present a report card to the teacher, which remains on the latter's desk throughout. At the end of the lesson, the teacher initials the card if the child has produced the necessary desirable behaviour, and if by the end of the week the child has had each lesson initialled then he or she is taken off report.

The disadvantages of the report card as a performance contract are that the child has very little say in the terms of the contract, and may be unclear as to the precise forms of behaviour expected. Different teachers in different lessons may in any case interpret what is meant by these behaviours rather differently, and the 'reward' available at the end of a successful period of being on report may be insufficient as an inducement. To be really effective, a performance contract will take account of each of these factors.

Briefly what happens with such contracts is that the headteacher or other appropriate senior member of staff meets the child and in an informal, supportive interview discusses specific ways in which the latter's behaviour could be improved, and specific ways in which the school could more effectively be meeting the needs of the child. It might be for example that the child's behaviour could be improved by not missing lessons without proper excuse, by turning up for lessons on time, and by handing in work promptly. The child agrees that each of these behaviours is a realistic proposition, and undertakes to produce them for, in the first instance, a specified period of time (perhaps only a week to begin with).

In return, the school promises that the child will be given a specified amount of extra help with school work, or will be allowed to re-enter a project or a special privilege from which bad behaviour has excluded him or her, or that some other reasonable and desirable facility will be extended. Both headteacher (and other members of staff closely involved) and child sign the contract, and progress is reviewed by all concerned in another meeting at the end of the week.

It is also a good strategy to involve parents or the community in general in the contract. This has the advantage of making available a much wider range of desirable rewards for the child. It also increases parental involvement in the child's progress, and where the child's uncontrolled behaviour has also included vandalism outside school, it gives the community a chance to protect their own interests as well as materially to help the child's wider social integration. Examples of parental and community involvement might be that the parents will agree to give the child a special treat for which he or she has been asking, or to buy a particular gift. The community, in the form perhaps of a local garage or shopkeeper or (where possible) a sports club or a riding school will agree to allow the child to have the use of certain facilities and to help with certain routine but enjoyable tasks. Note that it is better if these parental and community rewards take a one-off or short-term form. In the case of parents in particular, it is far better to provide a single treat than to agree to a long-term rise in pocket money, since if the latter privilege has to be withdrawn due to a failure to keep the contract after it has been renewed a few times, this will inevitably lead to ill-feeling between parents and child. Far better that each time the contract is renewed it carries a reward which can be seen by both parties as tied specifically to that contract, and which cannot come rapidly to be accepted by the child as a right rather than as a privilege.

Each time the contract comes to be successfully renewed, the child can be given a little more responsibility for its formulation and for the variables to which it refers. Thus the controls over his or her behaviour come increasingly to be seen by the child as something involving him or herself as well as other people. The child therefore becomes more committed to seeing that these controls operate successfully. Instead of being always imposed by outsiders, they are now dependent in part upon his or her own decisions and judgement.

In spite of the successful operation of the performance contract within education, many teachers object strongly to it as a strategy for classroom control. They argue firstly that the school cannot go on operating a contract with individual children indefinitely, and secondly that such a contract is unfair (and will be seen to be unfair) by other children who are producing desirable behaviours without special rewards. Let me take these points in turn.

It is certainly difficult to go on operating a contract indefinitely with particular children, but this is where the notion of *incidental reinforcement* comes in. While producing the specified behaviours and being rewarded for them a child is also finding that a range of other desirable consequences which are not mentioned in the contract are accruing. By keeping their part of the contract and producing better behaviours in class, children who are on performance contracts find that not only do they receive the specified extra help from the teacher, but that general relationships with the teacher improve and that they begin to experience success in academic work and to understand and become interested in lessons. Their improved performance in school may also bring praise from parents, while other children will stop seeing them primarily as troublemakers and will start responding to them in more relaxed and friendly ways. While enjoying the privilege of helping out at the local garage or riding stable on Saturday morning they begin to learn more about the skills involved and perhaps to make themselves sufficiently useful to the proprietor for the latter to want to keep them on after the end of the contract and to start allowing them more responsibilities. Incidental reinforcers of this nature will serve to maintain children's improved behaviour after the end of the contract, as they begin to discover that socially acceptable behaviour *in itself* serves to bring desirable rewards and to open up not only new experiences but new ways of relating to oneself and to other people.

On the second issue of whether other children will think it unfair for one child to receive extra privileges simply for producing the kind of behaviours that they produce as a matter of course, the answer is that these other children will already be enjoying many of the reinforcers that are built into the contract. Through their co-operative classroom behaviour they will already be experiencing success; indeed if they are not, then the school should ask itself very seriously what has been going wrong. They should already be receiving within their home background many of the 'treats' that the more deprived child is now earning through the successful operation of a contract. These children will therefore have little cause to envy the child who is now receiving these things through sticking to the terms of a formal contract.

A good performance contract should:

1. Set attainable standards and involve the child in having from the start some say in what the contract contains.
2. Be agreed and signed by all the parties concerned.
3. Carry desirable and realistic rewards (and specify desirable and realistic child behaviours).
4. Run for short periods and be renewable, so that the child can see clearly the progress he or she is making and obtain rewards at frequent intervals.
5. Involve parents and the community where possible.
6. Be interpreted consistently by all staff involved.

7. Make absolutely clear to the child the kinds of behaviour desired and how they will be recognized by teachers as they occur.
8. Allow the child to take a little more responsibility for the terms of the contract as it comes up for renewal each time.
9. Carry ample opportunities for the operation of incidental reinforcers.

Types of classroom punishment

Turning now from classroom rewards to classroom punishments, it simplifies matters to point out that for the most part effective punishments consist primarily in withholding the rewards that I have just been discussing. The absence of teacher attention and of teacher praise and teacher encouragement, the failure to win good results, house points and privileges, are all in themselves a potent form of punishment. Where the child comes from a home in which success at school is particularly prized and emphasized, the absence of such tokens of this success will cause added concern and anxiety, and will act as an effective shaping influence upon the child concerned. But there are, nevertheless, occasions when teachers may feel that something even more direct is required.

Particularly with younger children, the expression of disapproval for a child's behaviour is often sufficient. The teacher points out that the behaviour is unacceptable, and tells the child why. However, as we have already seen, for some children any teacher attention may be seen as rewarding, either because the child is unable to obtain this attention by good behaviour or because making the teacher angry or stop what he or she is doing and attend to the child reinforces the latter's sense of personal power and significance. Accordingly, the teacher may turn to some more concrete sanction.

Before discussing what this sanction might be, and whether or not it is likely to be effective, the general point needs to be made that concrete punishments per se are not a very successful or desirable method for controlling chidren's behaviour. This is for the following major reasons:

1. The effect of the kind of punishment available to teachers tends to be temporary. The behaviour that has been punished is only suppressed in the short term, and will recur in many cases once the punishment is discontinued or the child becomes accustomed to it.
2. Punishment often leads simply to more subtle evasive tactics on the part of the child, who learns to develop strategies for hiding

responsibility for unwanted behaviour, strategies such as lying and subterfuge.

3. By punishing a child, the teacher is directly attacking the relationship of mutual respect and friendliness that he or she is aiming to create with the child.

4. When punishment is handed out, the teacher inevitably is drawing attention to bad behaviour. Research indicates that it is more effective to draw attention to wanted behaviour than to unwanted. Thus a word of praise for good behaviour, or a request for quiet work, are preferable to a condemnation of bad behaviour or a command to stop all the noise.

5. Punishment helps arouse negative feelings in the child about the context in which such punishment takes place. He or she will therefore often come to dislike and avoid the teacher concerned, and perhaps also to dislike the subject the teacher teaches and even the room in which that teaching takes place.

6. Punishment, particularly when seen to be arbitrary and unfair, teaches the lesson that it is acceptable for the strong to make victims of the weak.

7. There is always the danger that, perhaps above all in children who are particularly oriented towards the need to do well, fear of punishment will curb originality and creativity. The desire to avoid punishment may lead such children to show excessively conformist and 'safe' behaviours even on occasions when the school believes itself to be deliberately encouraging initiative.

With these reservations very strongly in mind, it is apparent that concrete punishments must be seen by the children as consistent and fair in their application, and to be suited to the particular offences at which they are directed. And of vital importance, they should be thought of as a means of correcting future behaviours rather than as a form of revenge against the child. Thus they should always include some way of helping the child see where he or she has gone wrong and what can be done from now on to put things right.

The headteacher's letter. One good example of this, and indeed one of the most effective sanctions available to the school, is the headteacher's letter to parents. By writing a letter home, and pointing out to parents where a child has been at fault and how this fault can be remedied, the school is directly influencing the child's family relationship. Very few parents are completely indifferent to their child's progress at school, and many of them will take issue with a son or daughter who has been creating a bad impression with teachers. The best way of using the letter to parents is by incorporating it into what could be called a modified performance contract. The headteacher writes the letter, and then calls the child in and reads it out loud. The letter points out calmly and factually and in necessary detail exactly what the child has been up to and how teachers have reacted in consequence, and the child is asked if the letter should be sent.

If the child says no, he or she is asked what specific improvements in behaviour can be offered in order to dissuade the headteacher from putting it in the post. Once these are agreed between headteacher and child, the former places the letter on the file, with the understanding that it will be sent (together with an addition to the effect that the child cannot keep his or her word) if the agreed behaviour is not forthcoming. For a specified period, the child then has to report to the headteacher regularly to discuss progress, and if all goes well the letter is given to the child at the end of this period to be destroyed there and then. This effectively means that the child is being given a new start, with the proviso that another letter can be prepared if behaviour relapses.

Time-out. The use of a letter to parents is something of which all staff should be aware, and on which they should all be agreed. The same is true of most systems of punishment. To be effective, they need to be seen as part of school policy, supported by the whole staff and not just operated in isolation by individuals. This is particularly true of a sanction which is now graced with the name *time-out* (or 'time-out from positive reinforcement', to give it its full title). Time-out means that the child is removed from the context in which the undesirable behaviour is occurring. It will be recalled that I stressed the importance of *context* earlier in the chapter. A child may be misbehaving through the need to obtain the attention of the teacher or of the rest of the class. Remove the child from the context in which this attention is being sought (i.e., remove the child from the classroom) and the possibilities of gaining this attention will disappear, and along with them the stimulus for producing the misbehaviour.

Teachers, of course, have long operated a kind of time-out when they have sent a child to stand outside the classroom, but this rather crude strategy has obvious drawbacks in that the child may miss half the lesson while the teacher (unintentionally or otherwise) forgets about him or her. Or the child may alleviate boredom by pulling faces at classmates through the glass partition, or may simply decide to go off home. Time-out attempts to avoid these consequences by systematizing the whole procedure.

A small time-out room is provided, supervised either by the head-teacher in a primary school, or in the secondary school by a member of staff who is free for that period and who is known for his or her effectiveness in keeping order. The child is sent to the time-out room for a specified period of time (usually no more than five or ten minutes) and sits there under the watchful eye of the teacher concerned. The room is bare of stimuli, and the child experiences a rather boring interlude before being allowed to rejoin the class. If unwanted behaviour is repeated, then the child is returned to the time-out room for another spell.

At first the visits to the time-out room may be something of a novelty, but this novelty quickly wears off, and the child comes to miss the potential stimuli and attention available in the classroom. If he or she has been interrupting the work of the class, the class may also find that things are much more pleasant and they learn more when the former is out of the room. In consequence instead of being amused by the child's antics the class may now view them with some displeasure, and in consequence there may now be some pressure from peers upon the child to conform as well as from the teacher.

A variant of time-out is for teachers to be formed into small groups within the school, with each member using the other individuals within the group as a resource. Thus, a child who misbehaves may be sent from one classroom to sit in with another. Here the child is something of an outsider, with little chance of gaining the kind of initiative that is enjoyed with peers, and in consequence is glad when the time comes to go back where he or she belongs. Another example is where the child is sent to sit in with the deputy head-teacher, who perhaps has a special responsibility for discipline. Note that on none of these occasions does the teacher to whom the child is sent try to 'lecture' the latter or ask for explanations. The child is simply told to sit in silence while the teacher gets on with his or her own work. If the child persists in fidgeting or trying to talk, the period spent in the time-out room is lengthened, though it is made clear to the child that work which has been missed in his or her own classroom will have to be completed, which may involve, for example, staying behind to complete any tests or other such exercises which have taken place.

Beyond the withholding of teacher attention and approval, the withdrawal of privileges, the placing on report or on a performance contract, the letter to parents, and the operation of time-out there are few punishments likely to be effective. Detention and impositions are little more than a minor irritation for most children, unless they are so swingeing as to take up a great deal of their time (which raises the issue of whether it is a good thing for them to be constrained to spend such time in unproductive pursuits). Depriving them of games is an unjustifiable interference with an essential part of education, and likely to raise the righteous wrath of the physical education staff if it is done at secondary school level. Giving extra homework or extra tasks in subjects like mathematics only prompts them to associate these things with punishment. And corporal punishment does more harm to the relationship between teacher and child than it contributes towards improving behaviour; in any case it is rapidly ceasing to be an option for most teachers.

The law of natural consequences. Finally, something that is not really inflicted by the school at all, but is in fact inflicted upon children themselves. We can refer to it as the 'law of natural consequences', and it means quite simply that the child is allowed to experience the consequences of his or her own actions. Clearly, this is a highly effective form of modifying behaviour. If we treat our tape recorder roughly for example, it breaks and we then have to do without it. If we are late when we are called to do something, we miss our turn and have to wait until last. Assuming we enjoy using our tape recorder and do not like losing our turn, then we will modify our behaviour accordingly in the future. Unfortunately from the point of view of behaviour modification, though fortunately from the point of view of personal safety and humanitarian principles, we are frequently not left to experience the consequences of our own misdeeds. Other people intervene to protect us from them. The broken tape recorder is replaced by a kind parent; the others wait to let us have our turn after all. We are not left to suffer injury when we misuse equipment or apparatus, or to go without food because we have not helped in buying or preparing it. The result, however, of this kindness is that the full reality of the situation often does not become apparent to us, and we go on making the same mistake over and over again.

From the school point of view, the operation of the law of natural consequences can have only limited scope. Not only has the school to ensure children's safety and to provide them with appropriate educational opportunities, it also has the rights of the rest of the class to take into account. However, within obvious and very carefully defined limits, natural consequences can be allowed to serve as a way of helping shape behaviour and retain control over individuals and groups. For example, the nursery or infant school child who breaks a toy or a piece of play equipment through misuse can experience for a short time what it means to have to do without it. Similarly, the child who rudely declines the teacher's offer of help, once more for a short time can be left to experience what it means to struggle along on your own. Of if children leave unnecessary litter after completing an activity they can be asked to clear it up. Or if they abuse the teacher's trust when given a certain privilege, then they can be required to forfeit the privilege. In all these examples, it is important that the natural consequences are experienced by the child as soon as possible after the activity which brought them about. In this way he or she is helped to see the causal link between the two, and is thus more likely in future to refrain from the activity concerned.

It is also important that teachers do not attempt to reinforce the natural consequences by delivering strong verbal rebukes. They may feel it necessary to draw the child's attention to the link between cause and effect, but if a lengthy vilification of the child is then attempted the latter's attention may be distracted from this link or he or she may be left resentful and hostile. Far better to let the natural consequences speak for themselves, merely pointing them out to the child in a brisk and matter-of-fact way. The child is then left with the clear awareness that these consequences have been brought upon him or herself, rather than being decreed as a result of an angry decision on the part of the teacher.

Negative reinforcement. Before leaving this discussion of punishment within the context of the behavioural approach, I should make clear the distinction in behavioural terminology between 'punishment' and 'negative reinforcement'. Many students and teachers assume that since 'positive reinforcement' is another term for reward, then 'negative reinforcement' must be another term for punishment. This is not so. 'Negative reinforcement' refers to the removal of punishment or of other undesirable consequences, such removal in itself being a way of modifying behaviour. Suppose for example a child has been punished each time for owning up to a misdemeanour of some kind. In the end, to avoid this punishment, the child develops the frequent strategy of lying or of carefully covering tracks so that discovery is unlikely. If we now remove the punishment, or reduce it markedly in severity as a recognition of the child's honesty on the occasions when the truth is told, then the lying and the deviousness will tend to decrease. Through negative reinforcement, the child will have learnt that telling the truth does not invariably lead to punishment, and if we now reinforce this by actively giving rewards for telling the truth (praise and commendation for example) then we may well have played a significant part in making the child into an honest person.

As this example shows, negative reinforcement, particularly when backed up by positive reinforcement, is at times an effective strategy in changing behaviour. But it often demands a teacher who is prepared to think carefully about what is actually happening when children are being punished. The disadvantages of punishment have already been listed, and by thinking these through carefully, the teacher can often see that the best strategy for class control may well simply be to discontinue the standard punishments that have hitherto been handed out for certain offences. In order to stop children cheating in class tests, for example, the best strategy might be to discontinue berating these children publicly for their poor performance (a bad strategy in any case). The cheating is in fact simply a device resorted to by the children to avoid humiliation in front of the rest of the class. And to stop a class responding negatively to a teacher, the best strategy might be to stop nagging the children for their inadequacies when compared to the class last year. The nagging has simply convinced the children that nothing they do is right, so as a result they have simply given up bothering to try. In these and other similar cases, the teacher is by a misapplication of punishment actively discouraging the kind of behaviours that are wanted from the class, and encouraging those behaviours that most need to be eliminated.

The behavioural approach to group problems

So far in this chapter I have discussed the behavioural approach mainly in the context of managing behaviour problems in individuals. But this approach also has much to say about working with groups of children and with the whole class. The principles remain the same here as when working with individual children. That is the teacher studies carefully the *behaviour* which needs changing in a particular group or in the whole class, the usual *consequences* of that behaviour, and the *context* in which it takes place.

The behaviours may be too much noise, excessive out-of-seat movement, antagonisms and hostilities between various groups or between certain children, refusal to obey teacher instructions, and so on. The consequences may be the teacher's own response (anger, pleading, shouting, scorn, threatening, etc.) or the responses of other children within the class, and the context may be a particular task set by the teacher, a particular time of day, the equipment which the children are being asked to use, the room in which the lesson is taking place, the seating arrangements, or a range of other similar variables. The teacher lists each item of behaviour, together with the consequences and the context, and then uses the list as a way of understanding precisely why things have been going wrong. Hostilities between two children or between two groups of children (the item of behaviour) may, for example, be seen to provide a degree of relief (the consequence) for the children concerned from a rather tedious section of the lesson (the context). Or disobedience towards the teacher on the part of a group within the class may be a way of obtaining similar relief by unsettling or angering the teacher. Or an uproar at the start of the lesson may be a way of delaying proceedings, or of rewarding the children by demonstrating their power over the teacher or over those of their number who are interested in the teacher's material and are anxious to get on with things.

As with individual behaviours, once the teacher understands more clearly why children are behaving as they do, steps can be taken to alter either the consequences or the context associated with that behaviour in order to modify it in desired directions. Consequences and context are discussed presently, but first it is necessary to emphasize that groups are of course made up of individuals; thus by working on the behaviour of individuals in the manner outlined in this chapter, the teacher will also be working upon the behaviour of the whole group.

As I made clear in Chapter 2, the behaviour of the group is often particularly influenced by leaders and stars within that group. Such children are sometimes referred to as 'gatekeepers', in the sense that they guard the way to entry into the group by an outsider. Once the outsider has gained the approval of the gatekeeper, then he or she will be allowed access to the group, and will be able to take more part in shaping group behaviours. In the classroom, this means that if the teacher identifies and relates well to the gatekeeper or gatekeepers, the problems of class control become much less. The rest of the class will tend to take their cue from the gatekeepers, and if the latter are seen to accept and co-operate with the teacher, then such acceptance and co-operation will tend to become the class norm, with class disapproval extended towards those children who fail to accept this norm.

Consequences and group behaviours. In many instances, careful analysis by the teacher will reveal that, as with individuals, it is his or her own behaviour that is tending to reinforce undesirable class or group responses. I have already given some examples of this, and the discerning teacher will quickly be able to add to these. It is an unfortunate fact of school life that a class of children will often take great (some teachers would say sadistic) pleasure in observing the discomfiture of a teacher. The teacher who fails to operate apparatus effectively, who becomes flustered and loses the place in lesson notes, who frequently makes mistakes and slips of the tongue, who confuses children's names, who becomes ineffectually angry and utters absurd threats, and who exhibits the range of behaviours to which I drew attention in Chapter 3, is viewed by children as a diverting spectacle. This failure to control the class appears to be a powerful reinforcer to further disruptive behaviour, not just because children are able to get away with such behaviour without effective punishment, but because they often enjoy witnessing this failure.

Having identified the teacher behaviours that appear to be acting as reinforcers for unwanted class activities, the next step is to change these behaviours. Again, as with individual behaviours, the teacher can draw up a hierarchy of the unwanted activities in question, and try to modify the least difficult ones by behavioural strategies first. If these strategies prove successful, this will render working on the more difficult ones rather easier, and will also give the teacher valuable experience and confidence in how to go about it. At the same time, positive reinforcement in the form of rewards should be given to the *wanted* behaviours. And here indeed working with the whole class is rather easier than working with individuals, since there are usually more opportunities for such reinforcement and for shaping generally. There will always be occasions when the class is working more quietly than usual, when they respond particularly well to a lesson, when they arrive punctually and settle down quickly, when they show co-operation, when they behave responsibly, and when they produce extra-good results. By praising and encouraging the class on these occasions, by rewarding them with privileges such as extra sessions of activities they particularly enjoy, by taking the opportunity to commend them as a class publicly to other members of staff, by introducing new and exciting areas of work made possible by the children's responsible attitude, the teacher can strongly reinforce these desirable behaviours.

Further group reinforcers. Further reinforcement can be provided by always drawing attention where possible to wanted behaviour rather than to unwanted. I have already touched upon this point, and what it means in practical terms is that the teacher tells the class what is wanted rather than telling them what they should not do. 'Look at the board' is therefore preferable to 'stop looking out of the window', 'work on your own' is better than 'stop chattering', 'put your hands up' is better than 'don't call out', 'answer politely' is better than 'don't be rude', and so on. Stressing wanted behaviour rather than condemning unwanted helps to establish these behaviours in the children's minds, and to indicate to them that the teacher is confident that they are capable of such behaviour. Where appropriate, and particularly if the children concerned have been identified privately by the teacher as gatekeepers, the attention of the class can be drawn to individuals who are manifesting the desired behaviour, and these children can then serve as models upon which the behaviours of the rest can be based. Needless to say, this is very much preferable to drawing the attention of everyone to those children who are not doing as they have been asked.

Other ways of rewarding the class are to switch activities before children begin to find them boring, to extend the process of decision-making where possible to the whole class as a recognition of their responsible behaviour (I say more about this in the next chapter), and to provide tangible evidence of progress in the desired directions. This last is particularly important with primary school children. If the teacher is, for example, trying to encourage the handing in of work on time, a chart may be put up marking in colour with a chosen symbol those days on which work comes in to order. By prior agreement with the class, it will be recognized that if a certain number of symbols appear within a given period of time, then the class will be allowed a special treat of some kind. A similar strategy can be used if the teacher is trying to encourage tidiness in the class, or quiet work in a particular lesson. Sometimes the class can be divided into groups, and a degree of friendly rivalry introduced between the groups, with each group represented by a different symbol on the chart.

The use of negative reinforcement. In addition to providing positive reinforcement, the teacher can also make use of negative reinforcement. I gave examples of this when discussing negative reinforcement a little earlier. Other examples are that a teacher's sarcasm and attempts to humiliate the class may have provoked the children into fighting back by rudeness and disobedience in order to express their anger and protect their self-esteem. An end to the sarcasm and rudeness may end the children's aggressive response. Or a teacher's unfairness and propensity for arbitrary punishment may have aroused the children's sense of injustice and led them to take every opportunity to make life difficult. A more equable approach on the teacher's part may lead the children to behave more reasonably in their own turn.

Reinforcement by the class. However, sometimes unacceptable behaviours seem to be sustained not by what the teacher does as a consequence of them, but by the doings of the rest of the class. One useful way of considering these doings is to see them as either overtly supportive or overtly hostile. Both, in the context in which they are discussed here, are reinforcing in that they are the sought-for consequences, but the teacher's methods for dealing with them will not be identical in each case. Supportive actions by the class cover those activities which express a friendly response to the unacceptable behaviours concerned. This response may take the form of smiles or appreciative laughter, or of verbal approval or encouragement. The child responsible for the original behaviour may react by continuing with or repeating the behaviour, and very quickly the whole class or a large group within the class may become involved. The options open to the teacher in terms of personal response are:

(a) to ignore the behaviour
(b) to reprimand the child responsible for the disturbance
(c) to reprimand the class
(d) to join in the general response.

Of these four options, option (a), as when ignoring individual children, may often be the most effective. This is certainly the case if the behaviour concerned is of a very minor kind, and the teacher judges that, if attention is not drawn to it, it will quickly subside. The choice between options (b) and (c) depends upon the identity of the child and children concerned and on the nature of the behaviour. In general singling out the ringleader of a class disturbance and instructing him or her by name to behave correctly is better than a general appeal for order, but the exception may arise if the child is a recognized troublemaker. Should this be the case, it is preferable not to draw further attention to him or her (which is probably what the child wants) but instead to direct controlling remarks to the whole class, indicating perhaps disappointment that they could allow themselves to act so foolishly. Option *(d)* is sometimes required when there has been a joke at the teacher's expense, and the laughter of the class indicates in fact that it is a very good joke. Far better to acknowledge this with a relaxed smile, and to pass on to other business than to show by resentment or anger that the joke actually hurt in some way.

Where the children's response to each other is hostility, with one group goading another, the teacher's preferred strategy depends in part upon an assessment of the consequences that arise from this goading. Are the children arousing each other simply as a way of upsetting the teacher or of enlivening a dull lesson? Or is there some real animosity between the groups of children concerned, perhaps having its origins beyond the classroom? If the former, then once more the teacher needs to look to his or her own behaviour. Why is it that the class enjoys upsetting the teacher? Or why is it that they find the lesson dull? But if it is the latter, then the remedy may lie outside the teacher's hands. Certainly the teacher will want to try talking things through with the children concerned and separating the children physically by moving one group to the other side of the classroom, but it may be that the problem will continue to recur until the children move on to another class or until there is a realignment of friendships within or across the groups concerned. .

Context and group behaviours. I discussed in Chapter 3 the various factors within the school or within the class that might provide the kind of context in which behaviour problems occur. These factors included organizational variables and physical variables, together with teacher and lesson content variables, and there is no necessity to run through them again. But if the teacher is sensitive to these variables, then they can be manipulated where possible to remove the circumstances that seem to give rise to trouble.

For example, if disruptive class behaviour seems to be a way of delaying the start of the lesson, lesson content can be reorganized so that the lesson always starts with something of interest, such as new information or a striking visual aid. If disruption occurs at the end of a lesson, primarily because the business of clearing up is left until very late, then the remedy is to stop work a little earlier and allow clearing up to take place in good time. If the classroom is badly arranged, and one group of children has to disrupt another in order to get to a particular piece of appratus or equipment (a common problem in primary schools or in craft and science lessons), then the classroom can be rearranged accordingly.

If much of the children's unwanted behaviour is directed towards an ill-considered school or classroom rule, then attention can be given to changing the rule. If children run in corridors because they are given insufficient time between lessons, or if they leave litter because there are inadequate litter bins, or break windows because they are forced through inadequate space to play too near the school building, or leave books at home because they are made to carry all their belongings with them all day, or carry out noisy protests because there is inadequate machinery for making their views known by acceptable means, then the remedies clearly lie in the main with the school itself.

Objections to the behavioural approach

Enough has been said in the present chapter to indicate that the behavioural approach can be a very useful way of dealing with problems of class control. As I show in Chapter 5 and in subsequent chapters it is only one way, however, and should be used in conjunction with other strategies rather than instead of them.

Nevertheless, in spite of its usefulness, some teachers are reluctant to consider the use of the behavioural approach, and muster a number of objections to it. These can be summarized and perhaps refuted as follows.

Behaviourism fails to take into account the fact that children are able to see what is going on and may be aware of the teacher's attempts to modify their behaviour by behavioural means.

This is true, of course. And there would be very few behaviourists these days who would be foolish enough to deny it. Children are often well aware of what is going on, and may deliberately choose to continue with a particular piece of behaviour in spite of the teacher's impeccable behavioural strategies simply as a way of confounding him or her. However, for the most part children have little incentive to be this devious. If behaviour that in the past has brought a desirable reward now no longer yields that reward, then they are likely to abandon it in favour of something more productive.

Behaviourism is somehow inhuman, and involves manipulating people against their will.

Behaviourists insist, reasonably enough, that from birth onwards the individual and the group are subjected to rewards and punishments from those around them. The problem is, they claim, that in the world at large such rewards and punishments are frequently ill-conceived and inconsistently and ineffectually applied. From the teacher's point of view, therefore, the behaviourist approach need simply be seen as a way of making these rewards and punishments into a more efficient and therefore productive system.

Behaviourism is all right in theory but in the classroom at least
it won't work in practice. You cannot for example just ignore
bad behaviour.
This is a fair point. But the answer is to concentrate initially only
upon those behaviours that appear to lend themselves more readily
to a behavioural technique. The others can be tackled by such a
technique later, when success has already been achieved at the more
basic level and where this success in itself is beginning to influence
more complex or more difficult behaviours.

Special skills are needed to operate a behavioural approach.
I have already tackled this one. All that the teacher needs is careful
and systematic observation, the readiness to change his or her own
behaviours in response to the facts revealed by this observation, and
the persistence to carry a behavioural programme through. All these
are professional skills which the teacher will already possess.

Behavioural techniques will only work well if all staff within
the school employ them.
This is a valid point in that to be effective behavioural techniques
should be applied consistently. Within the primary school the
individual teacher may use these techniques with his or her own
class usefully enough irrespective of the methods adopted by
colleagues, but in the secondary school it is obviously desirable that
all teachers with whom a child comes into contact should employ
common strategies. This does not mean that individual secondary
school teachers should not use the behavioural approach if this is
not general policy: simply that it is much better if staff see control
problems as affecting them all, and work out a school policy on the
approach to such problems which is understood, accepted and
operated by all (see Chapter 5).

Behavioural techniques threaten the relationship between
teacher and child.
This links in with the point about behaviourism's alleged

inhumanity and implies that if the teacher is using the behavioural approach he or she will be acting towards children without humanity, warmth, and a sensitivity to their individual needs. I discuss these qualities in Chapters 5 and 7, and emphasize their crucial importance, but the behavioural approach in no sense precludes them. In fact by the stress that it places upon observing and understanding the behaviour of the individual child it should place the teacher in an even better position to make use of them and to demonstrate their use to the child.

In sum, therefore, if behaviourism is seen by the teacher as a useful tool, to be used together with other strategies of class control, there is no reason why any of the above objections should preclude its use. I return to behaviourism briefly from time to time in the next and in subsequent chapters to show how it can be linked in with and can be used to support the teacher's other approaches to class control. I also indicate how behaviourism itself can be enhanced if it is placed within the context of these other approaches.

Reference.

For the behaviourist approach to classroom control see: Walker, J.E. and Shea, T.M. (1980) (2nd edn) *Behaviour Modification: A Practical Approach for Educators.* St Louis and London: C.V. Mosby.

Chapter 5

Strategies
II: The Cognitive Approach

There is no necessary conflict between a cognitive approach to problems of class control and a behaviourist one. I said in Chapter 4 that the main concern of the behaviourist is with observable behaviour, and that the behaviourist does not speculate about the reasons and motives behind people's actions since these are not apparent to the observer. The behaviourist concentrates upon what people actually do and upon the context and the consequences of their actions rather than upon what goes on inside their heads. However he or she does not deny the importance of this mental activity. The point is simply that it is difficult to be precise about it, and that a very great deal can be done to guide and direct and reshape people's actions without taking it directly into account.

From the teacher's angle, behaviourism yields a range of very useful and readily applied strategies for obtaining class control. But, for all its alleged elusiveness, teachers are also vitally concerned with the child's mental activity, with his or her inner world of thoughts, motives, memories and emotions. When it comes to matters of class control, no teacher would wish to be confined just to the behavioural approach. Nor indeed would such confinement be a good thing. The cognitive approach, which focuses attention upon this inner world, has at least as much to contribute to strategies of class control as has the behaviourist, and it would be a very limited teacher who was not prepared to draw freely upon both. Sometimes the teacher will try first one approach and then the other, experimenting to see which is the more appropriate in the circumstances. On other occasions the two approaches will be used in conjunction. As long as teachers do not allow the one approach to confuse the other, either in their own eyes or in those of the child, then their eclecticism is likely to be to everyone's advantage.

Motivation, interest and life goals

The questions of motivation and of interest are of particular concern to the cognitive psychologist just as they are to the teacher. For both the psychologist and the teacher are aware that if levels of motivation and interest are high, then learning takes place much more readily than if they are low. Problems of classroom control, if they exist at all, will tend to stem from boisterous over-eagerness or from impatience at the teacher's inability to take the class along quickly enough or successfully enough rather than from antagonism, attention-seeking behaviour or boredom.

The problem, however, is how does one arouse motivation and interest, and the long-term life goals that arise from them? The answer lies in part in a term used frequently by teachers but all too rarely by psychologists, namely *relevance*. If children find work relevant to them, then they are likely to show interest in it and to present few problems of class control. And where such problems arise, the teacher needs to ask, as a priority question, why the children are not interested enough in their work to pay attention to it rather than to wish to disrupt the class. Why, to put it another way, does the work not appear relevant? And here the teacher needs to look firstly at the work itself and at how it is being presented to the class. To look, in fact, at his or her own behaviour (note how already a link between the cognitive and the behaviourist approach is becoming apparent). What is it about this teaching behaviour that is failing to make the class lesson relevant to children? And what can be done about it?

The question of relevance. At this point, we must remind ourselves what we mean by relevance, since the term is not always clearly explained by those who make most use of it. In the educational context, work that is relevant to children is work that helps them in obvious ways to make a success of their lives (see Chapter 1). It helps them variously to make a success of relating to the people who are important to them, in understanding and using skills which help them gain mastery over the physical environment, in identifying what it is they want to do with their lives in career and vocational terms, in helping them recognize their own abilities and strengths and further develop them, in helping them accept and value themselves as individuals, and ultimately in helping them see a meaning and purpose in their own and in other people's existence.

I indicated in Chapters 1 and 2, when discussing the child and the reasons why he or she may pose problems of class control, that children vary greatly from each other as a consequence of factors such as abilities, socio-economic background, age and sex. The result of this variation is that they will also differ from each other in what is and is not seen by them to have relevance. Earlier, for example, I talked about 'deferral of satisfaction', and suggested that a child from a so-called middle class home may have been brought up to see the value of this practice, whereas a child from a so-called working class home may not have been so brought up. In terms of relevance, therefore, the former child might readily understand that some apparently tedious work has to be gone through for the purposes of passing a future examination and one day obtaining a better job and is therefore relevant, while the second child might not understand this. Similarly a child of apparently low ability may not see the relevance of the vocational skills that the teacher is trying to teach, since he or she may consider that the chance of obtaining the necessary qualifications to enter the vocation concerned are virtually non-existent.

In Chapter 3, when discussing teacher behaviours and class control, I said enough to show that what the teacher may regard as relevant may not be so regarded by the child. This is true for skill learning, but it is also true for 'appreciation' lessons such as poetry, music and art. The poem that for the teacher may convey profound lessons about love or about beauty or about what it means to be human may mean little or nothing to the child. Not because the latter is incapable of being stirred by poetry, but because that particular poem uses language, imagery and concepts that are foreign to his or her own immediate experience. So it is with a piece of music or with a painting. The song or piece of orchestral music that meant so much to the teacher when at the age the class are now may strike few chords in them, while the painting that fills the teacher with awe may leave the class unmoved. By resenting the children's indifference, and by seeing this indifference as in some sense their fault, a wilful disobedience to appreciate qualities that are staring them in the face, the teacher will be inviting the control problems that spring from annoyance in some and apathy in others.

As Chapter 6 shows, part of the answer here lies in organizing the school and its curriculum in a manner that is responsive to the children's needs and that offers them relevance. But in terms of the individual teacher and the cognitive approach, the important point for the moment is that the teacher must try and see what kind of sense the experiences that are being offered actually make to the class. Are the children responding to and interpreting these experiences in the way in which the teacher wishes? Is it even possible for them to do so? Can the children see the application of these experiences (their relevance) to their own lives and to their daily concerns? Is the teacher looking for a response from the class which it is impossible for them to give? Has the teacher taken into account their levels of cognitive development in Piagetian terms and the other age and sex variables discussed in Chapter 1?

By understanding more clearly the way in which children are making sense or failing to make sense of the experiences offered them, the teacher is enabled to select and modify these experiences in such a way as to give them relevance, and thus to arouse interest and to increase the child's motivation to learn more. At this point the reader will find it helpful to turn back to Chapter 2 and to read again the variables discussed there. A central feature of the cognitive approach to problems of class control is that many of these problems can be prevented before they arise if the teacher studies children carefully and fully appreciates the variables that influence the way in which they conceptualize what is going on in the classroom. Has the child's background been an appropriate preparation for the values, standards and interests that the school is trying to teach? Is he or she able to identify with the school's aims and objectives? Does he or she perceive the teacher's efforts as a means of offering help or as a threat? Does school appear to offer him or her the real chance of success or simply the assurance of continual failure? Is the school curriculum a source of support and enjoyment and of broadening horizons or of tedium and frustration? In each of these instances, if things are seen by the teacher to be going wrong, the cognitive approach stresses that the teacher and the school must study ways of changing how they present themselves to the child, instead of automatically assuming that it is the child who is at fault and who must therefore be the one to make any changes that appear to be necessary.

Locus of control and self-monitoring

One of the most important areas within this context explored by the cognitive psychologist is that of *locus of control* . The term was first given prominence by Rotter and stands for whether the individual sees the events controlling his life as lying within or outside the self. Where the locus of control is *internal*, the individual tends to see the things that happen to him or her, for good or bad, as due to his or her own behaviour (e.g., 'I passed the exam because I worked hard',

'I forgot my books because I was in too much of a hurry', 'I'll do well at my music if I practise hard enough'). Where the locus of control is *external*, the individual tends to see things as a consequence of outside forces ('I made a mess of it because the teacher hadn't prepared us properly', 'If I get the right kind of help I'll do well', 'I was lucky and they asked me all the right questions').

Closely linked to the concept of locus of control is what is known as *attribution theory* which draws attention to the way in which people attribute the cause of the various things that happen to them in life. From the perspective of class control, the important implications of locus of control and of attribution theory are that if individuals feel they have some control over (and therefore some responsibility for) events, then they are more likely to persist in the kinds of behaviour that lead to success in school. They will be more likely to attend to work and to persevere in the face of difficulty and to co-operate with the people who prove themselves able to offer appropriate help. Attribution theory goes further and says that also important are the values attributed to a particular task. If these values are high, then a person will be prepared to continue with the task even though in itself its level of interest may not be high.

Research evidence indicates that an internal locus of control goes with satisfactory school achievement. If children are allowed to experience a degree of control over their learning environment, then they will learn more effectively. Obviously we have to be careful here. If by helping children to internalize their locus of control we lead them to believe that whenever they fail in anything it is in consequence their own fault, then we will be doing more harm than good. What the research really seems to show is that:

1. Children should be given realistic and appropriate opportunities to have their say in how they learn and in how the class is organized and run.
2. Children should be helped to judge objectively and fairly where a particular attribution actually lies. Who is actually responsible for particular events, and what can therefore be done to put these events to rights if they prove to have undesirable results?

Point 1 has essentially to do with a degree of classroom democracy, and with the readiness by the teacher to listen to individual children's points of view and to give them credit for knowing on occasions what is best for themselves. Point 2 has to do with developing discrimination and the ability to examine things without undue emotional involvement. At a practical level, the best way of achieving this is often for the teacher to show a readiness to examine his or her behaviour, to listen to the class should they have grounds for criticizing this behaviour, and to be seen to be ready to make the necessary adjustments in relevant areas of it. This is often a difficult task for the teacher, since it may involve matters of professional pride, and I return to it in Chapters 7 and 8.

Of great importance here is the language that the teacher uses. It is of little value asking children their point of view in terms and in a tone that will be interpreted by the latter as threatening. 'I don't suppose anyone can find fault with *that* can they?', issued in an intimidating voice while the teacher glowers round the classroom, will be interpreted by the children as really meaning, 'Don't anyone dare disagree'. And 'Last time we talked about this we were held up for ages by people who wanted to raise objections' will be interpreted as 'If anyone does that again I shan't bother consulting you in future'.

The demon effect and the self-fulfilling prophecy

Most teachers are familiar with what is called the 'halo' effect, that is, the phenomenon that if we are already impressed by someone's behaviour in one context then we will be favourably predisposed towards their efforts in another. What is not so often recognized is the opposite effect, sometimes termed the 'demon' effect, under which if we already have a bad impression of an individual then we are predisposed to interpret their future actions negatively. This is another way of reminding ourselves of the old adage that 'give a dog a bad name and someone is bound to hang him'. The very fact that a child is noted down as a troublemaker means that even innocent behaviours on his or her part tend to be viewed by us with suspicion, while if there is any group trouble going on in the vicinity we tend automatically to assume that he or she is in some way behind it. As a result, the child may well develop a sense of grievance against the teacher for always 'picking on me', and will in turn tend to interpret unfavourably even the teacher's reasonable overtures. Thus a spiral will be started in which both teacher and child will become more and more hostile towards each other and less and less inclined to give any credit where it in fact falls due.

The self-fulfilling prophecy. This is an example on both sides in fact of what is known as the self-fulfilling prophecy. If we prophesy that a child is going to turn out as a difficult member of the class, then we behave towards him or her accordingly, and the result of our behaviour is to risk producing those very difficult behaviours that we started off by prophesying. Similarly if a child forecasts that a teacher is going to be an enemy, then he or she may well react towards the latter in a sufficiently unfriendly way to ensure that the teacher after a while does indeed fall into this category.

Clearly what is required on the part of the teacher is the readiness to judge a child's behaviour on its own merits rather than in terms of presuppositions. It may be that the child has just moved into the teacher's class, bearing a bad reputation from a previous teacher or teachers. Having been told to 'watch out' for the child, the teacher must beware of the tendency to misinterpret the child in consequence or to give the impression that the latter is being singled out from the word go for special surveillance and worse still punishment. Now that the child is in a different class with a different teacher (and perhaps even taking a different subject) then the context in which the behaviour is taking place has been changed. It will be remembered from the discussion of the importance of context in Chapter 4 that this in itself may be sufficient to influence for the good the way in which the child goes about things.

It could be for example that there was a personality clash between the child and the teacher in the last class. As was made clear in Chapter 2, such clashes can be of great importance; for example, if they happen between an extra-lively child and a teacher who places special emphasis upon order and quiet in the classroom. Or it could be that the child found it difficult to understand the teacher's style of teaching, or found something about the teacher that was particularly irritating (see Chapter 3). Or it could be that the child had problems at home last year which were worrying but which have now eased (see Chapter 2), or that the child was with a group of children who tended to egg him or her on, or that there were immaturities then which have now disappeared. Whatever the reason, the child may be a very different proposition this year from last, and wise teachers draw their own cognitive 'maps' of the child, rather than taking over and sticking to the map handed on by a colleague or colleagues.

Self-concepts and self-esteem

In Chapter 3 I discussed in detail the importance for a child's classroom behaviour of self-concepts and evaluations. If children think of themselves as bad, perhaps because other people have consistently so described them, or if they think of themselves as failures, or as people whose learning problems are simply a nuisance to the teacher, then they are far more likely to cause class control problems than if they conceive of themselves as well-liked by teachers, as identified with success and therefore with the academic objectives of the school, and as people whose learning problems engage the professional interest of those responsible for them.

Part of the teacher's task in dealing with and preventing classroom control problems is to do everything possible to help children develop positive and success-oriented self-concepts. This means, to amplify the point that was first introduced in Chapter 1, that the child must be given the opportunity to experience academic success at his or her appropriate level. Praise and encouragement, designed to indicate to children that there are acceptable areas of their work that can be built on, plus the readiness always to set children work which is realistically within their competence will help them to redraw the cognitive maps that they have of themselves and of themselves in relation to school. Of equal importance, the friendliness of the teacher's own manner, and the readiness to indicate an interest in children and their work, will show to the latter that they are acceptable as human beings; that they are each somebody, in fact, who matters enough for the teacher to be pleased to see them and want to spend time offering them help. Realistically, of course, we have to accept that this is a tall order when it comes to certain children, but it is the teacher's professional and personal duty to make the effort. Once the effort is made, the improvements in the child's behaviour will often be sufficient reward to help the teacher keep trying.

Self-presentation

I have stressed in this chapter that the important aspect of the cognitive approach from the class control perspective is the *sense* that individuals make of the environment in which they are working. If they see the environment as being an important, supportive and interesting one, then they will identify with it and produce behaviours that are in conformity with it. If on the other hand they find the environment threatening, confusing and irrelevant, then they will refuse to identify with it and will tend not to produce the kind of behaviour that are in harmony with it. Since the teacher is a critically important part of this environment, then those remarks apply to him or her and not just to the curriculum and the examination system and the physical context and teaching strategies of the school itself. The teacher's self-presentation must be, therefore, likely to prove acceptable and professionally attractive to the children. This means self-presentation as someone who has knowledge, skills and abilities that the children would like to share, who is the kind of person they can get to know and like, and as the kind of person (of great importance) who can exercise sufficient class control to provide the structured framework within which they can successfully carry out their academic and social tasks.

In Chapters 6 and 7 I discuss the organizational and the personality qualities that help give children this favourable impression of the teacher. But there is a range of techniques relatively independent of organization and personality which are also of great importance and which the teacher can learn without too much difficulty. I will take each of these in turn, and attempt to indicate how they can help in the creation of the kind of desirable cognitive interpretation of the teacher by the children that leads to effective class control.

Confidence of manner. When we judge people, particularly for the first time, we go in part on the opinion that they appear to have of themselves. Confronted with a teacher who appears hesitant and unsure of the kind of reception he or she is likely to be given, the class will not unnaturally assume that here is someone who has experienced control problems in the past and is fearful lest they are likely to occur again. Confronted, on the other hand, by a teacher who seems poised and assured, the class is likely to assume that here is someone who is accustomed to obedience in dealings with children. Remember that in Chapter 2 'limit testing' was discussed, the tendency by children on first acquaintance with teachers to test out the limits beyond which they will not allow behaviour to go. It is easy to see that the former teacher will be extending a much more inviting invitation to the class to test limits than will the latter. What can the teacher who does not feel confident do, however? (There is nothing to be ashamed of in this.) The answer is either to act as if one does feel confident, or squarely to face one's fears and come to terms with them before meeting the class.

The latter is clearly the better strategy, and I discuss it fully in Chapter 8, but in the short term, the teacher may find it necessary to play the role of the confident teacher. Which means:

- being unhurried in one's speech and actions
- maintaining relaxed and non-threatening eye contact with the class and individuals
- being sure to avoid nervous mannerisms and gestures

- being ready to smile at the class as appropriate and join in any reasonable classroom laughter
- carefully avoiding unjustified antagonism or over-reaction to the children's behaviour.

Careful instructions and guidance. Problems of class control often arise because the children are puzzled as to what is really expected of them or what the teacher will allow and not allow. It is therefore very important that, particularly at the beginning of the lesson, or when changing from one activity to another, or when meeting a class for the first time, the teacher makes clear what is wanted from the class.

This should be done only when the teacher has the *full attention of the class* (see Chapter 7), and the instructions which are issued should be *brief, to the point, and couched in simple language.* The children should then be asked if they have any questions, and finally the teacher should ask 'Is everyone clear on what they have to do?'. The teacher then glances enquiringly around the class, holding eye contact and thus signalling that sensible doubts are invited from anyone, and then indicates that the class is to proceed.

If the class is a young or rather noisy one and the task involves movement around the room, then it is sensible to release the children one group at a time, thus enabling the teacher to call a halt to proceedings at once if need be. Once the children have a clear cognitive picture of what is required of them, they are likely not only to carry out their assignments more efficiently and with less disruption, they are also likely to perceive the teacher as an effective and decisive person.

Consistency and fairness. No map is of much use if the terrain to which it refers keeps shifting. If the child is to have a useful cognitive map of what goes on in the classroom and how to relate to the teacher, then *consistency* in the way in which the classroom is run and in the way in which the teacher conducts him or herself is vital. To operate in a successful way, the children need to know that the standards laid down by the teacher are not going to be subject to arbitrary and unexpected change, and that the teacher is not going to treat individual children differently from each other for no apparent reason, or fluctuate wildly in the treatment of the same child or of the whole class from day to day. This consistency on the part of the teacher also links in with the concept of fairness, upon which children appear to place so much emphasis (see Chapter 7).

Firmness in the face of problems. In Chapter 4 I discussed reasons why the teacher might choose to ignore certain recurrent behaviours in individuals and in groups. However, many behaviours are not part of a particular pattern, but instead either occur unexpectedly or as part of the range of variations that go to make up the teacher's day. Children who are not normally associated with disturbances may suddenly act uncharacteristically, or the class may go through a restless period half-way through the afternoon, or unexpected interruptions to the lesson from outsiders (a frequent hazard in the primary school) may act as a distraction. In such instances a firm word from the teacher at the outset, before things have time to build up into a major problem, is usually called for. This indicates to the class that the teacher is aware of everything that is going on in the room, can quickly decide whether something is acceptable or not, and is adamant that the reasonable standards under which work becomes possible are going to be maintained. There is no need for this firm word from the teacher to be a hostile one. A quick reminder to the child concerned or to the class is usually all that is needed. Should another reminder prove necessary, it is often better to back this up with some decisive physical gesture, such as moving the offending child to a seat nearer the front, or changing the class activity from, for example, working individually to a few minutes of quick classroom questions and answers (see Chapter 6).

The possibilities for quick, firm action of this kind are greatly enhanced if the teacher decides in advance when planning lessons what kinds of activities are likely to lead to problem behaviours, what form these behaviours are likely to take, and how bad the behaviour can become before it calls for teacher intervention. In this way the teacher is much less likely to be taken by surprise when things go wrong, and much less likely to act hesitantly or inappropriately when trying to put these things to rights. He or she is also less likely to include in the lesson any activities which are likely to prove obvious sources of trouble (see Chapter 6).

Awareness of what is happening. One of the essential qualities of the effective teacher is an alert awareness of what is going on in the classroom during the lesson. Thus the teacher is able to spot promptly when children are having difficulties with their work or when they are engaged in some clandestine and forbidden activity.

Such an alertness comes relatively easily to some people, particularly if they are interested and involved in the lesson and in their children. But it can be learnt readily enough by others. One essential aspect of it is that the teacher keeps as physically mobile as possible, moving around the room rather than attempting to conduct the lesson from a static position at the front of the class or behind the desk. Thus the children are aware that they are never out of sight for any length of time.

Another essential is that the teacher does not become trapped behind a little group of children all with individual questions while the rest of the class devotes itself seriously to the business of creating mayhem. This is a particular problem in the primary school, where children are all too ready to dog the teacher round the room, hands waving aloft, until they have manoeuvred him or her into a corner where further retreat becomes impossible. The response to such children must be that no one will have a query attended to unless they stay in their place with hand up and wait their turn. A third essential is that during the class lesson the teacher makes a point of relating to all the children in the room by, for example, directing questions at them and exchanging eye contact, rather than simply the small group at the front who appear to be showing most interest.

A knowledge of the children. In Chapter 2 I set out many of the major reasons why children may cause behaviour and class control problems. By familiarizing themselves with reasons of this kind, teachers are in a position to study children and make decisions on what can be reasonably expected from them and on what might best be done to remedy problems. By getting to know children individually, by becoming familiar with their backgrounds, their ability levels, their personalities, their previous experiences in school, and their relationships with the rest of the class, the teacher is in a much better position to exercise realistic and effective control strategies. A remark that might indicate calculated rudeness if made by one child, for example, may simply be made without thinking by another. A topic that may keep one child working happily all lesson may have little or no interest for another. Working conditions that may be ideal for some members of the class may be rather unsuitable for others. What might motivate one child might have no effect upon another. What might challenge and stimulate one child might frighten and daunt another. A remark that might amuse one child might be deeply wounding to another. What is simply high spirits with one child might be a deliberate attempt at disruption with another. And so on.

I am not suggesting here that the teacher should operate different standards when dealing with different children. In fact I have already stressed the importance of consistency. What I am saying is that the teacher should be sensitive to the individual characteristics of children, and should use this sensitivity in helping with the interpretation of children's behaviour and in avoiding both unnecessary confrontations with individuals and the situations that are most likely to lead to problems.

In addition to knowledge at this fundamental level, the teacher should also carry a store of more homely knowledge about the children in his or her class. Their personal likes and dislikes, their hobbies, their opinions and views on things. The possession of this knowledge demonstrates clearly to children the teacher's interest in them as people, and also provides ready topics of conversation when the teacher seeks to reward children with attention (see Chapter 4) or when meeting them outside the classroom. The teacher who is able to make good social contact with children outside the classroom is, in fact, less likely to meet with control problems than is the teacher who is awkward and embarrassed with these children when outside the usual professional context.

Of vital importance in this area is knowing children's names. Getting to know someone's name quickly and proving able to remember it is often a sign of our interest in them, and predisposes them to be more friendly towards us in turn. But in the classroom there is the added advantage that if the teacher knows the names of children, questions can be directed at them if their attention is wandering during the lesson, and they can be called by name if they are posing a problem of class control. The teacher who doubts this can experiment by calling a class to order by offering a general command, and next time attempt the same thing by calling out the name of an individual. On the first occasion the response is likely to be far less immediate than on the second. Even if in fact the child whose name was called was engaged in nothing more heinous than gazing out of the window, the whole class will at once stop what they are doing to look in his or her direction, giving the teacher the needed opportunity to insist that everyone gets down to work.

For the teacher who finds difficulty in remembering names, a seating plan of the class is essential. A (reliable) member of the class can be asked to draw up the plan, filling in each child's name in the position which he or she is occupying in the class, and the teacher then keeps the plan on the desk and refers to it as necessary. Needless to say it must be insisted that the children occupy the same desks each lesson until the teacher has had enough time to commit their names to memory.

Realistic standards. Following on from the teacher's knowledge of his or her children, there comes the setting of realistic and appropriate standards for the class, both in terms of academic work and social behaviours. If teachers set themselves expectations unrealistically high (or low, though this is perhaps a less common problem), then both they and the children become dispirited and frustrated. The teacher feels that the class is not trying its best, while the children feel that they are being nagged to produce work of which they are not capable. With the consequent deterioration in relationships, problems of class control are likely to become more and more prevalent. If the children feel to be experiencing nothing but failure, then damage to their self-esteem, with all the undesirable consequences that has for learning and class control, is likely to occur. Far better to set standards clearly related to what is possible with any particular class of children, and then to indicate clearly to them one's belief in their abilities and one's reasoned expectations of success.

Enjoyment of teaching. This is a somewhat nebulous variable, but one which nevertheless plays an important part in successful teaching and in the maintenance of good class control, namely the teacher's own enjoyment of his or her professional tasks. Such enjoyment usually goes with a liking for children and an enthusiasm and expertise in the subject one is trying to teach. Where a teacher conveys such liking and enjoyment to the class, the children are more likely to conceptualize him or her as engaged in a task that is important and worth doing, and are more likely in consequence to attach importance to this task themselves. A teacher who clearly enjoys teaching is also paying children a subtle compliment, and one which is likely to increase their feelings of self-worth and of academic confidence. And the teacher who takes pleasure in his or her work is also more likely to stimulate children's interest in the subject being taught and to avoid the range of class control problems that stem primarily from boredom and apathy.

Other cognitive factors

The emphasis in this chapter has been upon the way in which children conceptualize the teacher and his or her functions, and build up what I have called *cognitive maps*, that is, patterns of ideas that help them make their own kind of sense of the environment and that help determine the way in which they respond to this environment. In terms of class control, the task of the teacher lies in part in understanding these patterns and in ensuring that where possible they are in accordance with the kind of reality (aims, objectives, motives, interests) that is being presented to the class. If the children are able to accept this reality, and therefore to identify with and co-operate with what the teacher is doing, then many of the more common class control problems are likely to be prevented.

In addition, through a knowledge of their children, individual teachers are able to build up in turn an accurate cognitive map of the class, and ensure that their own behaviour is appropriate to this map. Their demands and expectations will be related to what the children can actually do, rather than to some arbitrary standards unconnected to their abilities, interests, and general background. Their teaching methods will take into account the children's individual differences, and the rewards and punishments that they offer will be of a kind likely to carry meaning for the class.

Threats and consequences. But there are a number of further considerations that teachers must bear in mind if they are to develop the sort of cognitive framework that we are discussing. They should for instance avoid threatening the class or individuals wherever possible, and ensure that when threats have to be uttered they are realistic ones and can be carried out. Wild threats that the children know can never be put into effect serve to lower the children's conception of the teacher as someone to be taken seriously. Similarly too frequent threats, or threats which are never put into effect in spite of the children's bad subsequent behaviour, also serve to weaken the teacher's position with the class, as do feeble threats quite unrelated to the tough-mindedness of the children concerned.

Closely linked to the problem of threats is that of *consequences.* If the consequences of a particular piece of class or individual behaviour are likely to be undesirable (e.g., loss of privileges through failure to keep one side of a bargain, parts of the examination syllabus that are not going to be covered as the class is wasting too much time, withdrawal of equipment because it is being misused) then these must be spelt out clearly to the class at the appropriate point. This is not presented in the form of a threat ('what I shall do if this behaviour continues'), simply as a statement of fact. In effect, it is a move on the part of the teacher to draw the attention of the class to the 'natural consequences' that were discussed in Chapter 4. If the class chooses to continue with its unsatisfactory behaviour, then the teacher makes it clear that the blame for the undesirable consequences lies squarely with them, or with those individuals within the class who are refusing to co-operate with the rest. It is not a decision on the part of the teacher that is involved, as with a threat, but a decision on the part of the class themselves.

Clear rules and procedures. Another allied consideration has to do with the presence in the classroom of *clear rules and procedures* (see also Chapters 1 and 6). The number of these rules and procedures should be kept to a minimum, since if there are too many of them the children are likely to forget half of them and categorize the teacher as a rather fussy person whose likes and dislikes are not to be taken that seriously. In addition, the teacher will find that a great deal of time is spent trying to enforce rules rather than helping the class with their learning. But such rules and procedures as do exist must be spelt out clearly, must be seen to be sensible and of general benefit, and must be adhered to by everyone, including the teacher. Where possible, the rules should be the subject of democratic debate, with the children themselves taking partial responsibility for their formulation and therefore for upholding them. This links back to the discussion earlier in the chapter of locus of control, while the systematic observance of the rules by everyone relates to my earlier emphasis on the importance of consistency if the children are to build up effective cognitive maps of the values and standards expected of them.

Empathy and imagination. Finally in this section, it is helpful if in addition to studying children's personalities and backgrounds, and therefore coming to an understanding of the reasons behind their behaviour, the teacher is actually able to enter imaginatively into their world. This may sound a very vague statement, which sits rather oddly with the cognitive emphasis of this chapter. Imagination, though we each of us experience it as part of our daily lives, and acknowledge its importance in creativity, is regarded by many as an imprecise and highly subjective process, and hardly one which the teacher can learn to use as an aid to classroom control.

But clearly, the more that teachers are able to think themselves into the cognitive world of their children, and see things from the children's particular vantage point, the better able are they to appreciate children's interpretations of the environment and the intentions which children have in relation to it. Knowing children, as I have stressed, is an essential part of this process, but there is still something more, which perhaps for want of a better term can be described as the feelings of childhood. How does it actually *feel* to be five years old, or 10 years old, or 15 years old? How does the world look? What are adults like? Do they seem menacing and remote, or helpful and friendly? Are they a source of frustration and fear, or of support and assistance? And what about the physical environment? Is it colourful and attractive, or drab and boring? Does it stimulate on a Monday morning, after a weekend off school, or does it depress and dishearten? And what about the lesson tasks? Are these interesting and challenging, likely to spark off ideas and the desire to know and to create, or are they tedious and routine, dragging out each minute of the lesson interminably? And does a class test or examination seem like a useful exercise, designed to pinpoint areas where further help from the teacher is needed and will be willingly given, or like a threatening and intimidating obstacle, where a poor performance will lead to recriminations, accusations and humiliation?

And how does the rest of the class look? Are they friendly or hostile, on the same side or ranged against you? And when an opportunity arises for breaking the rules or for having a giggle at the teacher's expense, is this really intended as a malicious act or simply as a way of enlivening things a little or showing off to your neighbours? And is the classroom a place where you are listened to and have some say in what goes on and in the conditions of learning, or is it a place where things always seem to be imposed from on high, with little patience or respect shown for your views or for those of your peers?

Imaginatively entering the world of the child, and trying to see things as the child does, is not a particularly demanding exercise. It starts with a simple cognitive process, that of memory. We take the opportunity, preferably when in a relaxed mood during a quiet few minutes at home, to think back to our own schooldays. We recall our own classroom at the time when we were the age our children now are. We recall the atmosphere, the emotions, the joys and the frustrations, the way we conceptualized our teacher or teachers, our attitudes and opinions, our response to textbooks and to particular teaching methods, our reactions when the teacher announced a class test, our reactions when we obtained poor results for this or for any other areas of work. We recall the way the classroom looked, the difficulties we had in explaining ourselves to the teacher when things went wrong, the outrage at being wrongly punished for something for which we were not responsible, and the sense of impotence when the teacher refused to listen to our protestations. We recall friends, and the pleasure of surreptitious laughter at the back of the class, and the awful feeling of forgetting to do homework, and the hilarious experience of watching a teacher make absurd mistakes or fail to deal with simple problems. We also recall feelings of regret at angering or upsetting a teacher of whom we were fond, and our inability to convey these feelings to the teacher, or adequately to thank a teacher who had given special help, or who we admired and respected in a particular kind of way.

By this process of recall, the teacher sees the world which his or her children inhabit in a different light, and is able to place a reasoned and more accurate interpretation upon many class control problems. What seemed like deliberate provocation from a child, or like base ingratitude, or like callous irresponsibility, or like a rejection of friendliness, may in fact be simple analogies of those occasions in our own childhood when the teacher misinterpreted our actions through a refusal to listen to our attempted explanations, and thus created a classroom confrontation where none was in fact necessary. It allows the teacher, as I will discuss in Chapter 8, to remain calm and objective in many of those situations where otherwise anger and outrage might well up at what looks, on first sight, to be a calculated threat by a member or members of the class to the teacher's position of classroom authority.

The cognitive approach: an overview

As this chapter has raised a range of issues, it is appropriate now to draw them together and ensure that the practical implications involved are clearly understood. To start with, the teacher lays down clear guidelines as to what is expected of the children and why. As in the behavioural approach, these are expressed in positive rather than negative terms (what we do rather than what we do not do). Whether these are general guidelines which apply throughout the year, or whether they are simply related to what is to be done in a particular lesson, the children must be sure of their role and of that of the teacher, and aware of the consequences if these guidelines are not observed. With younger children, the teacher may wish to write down these guidelines on notices and display them at appropriate places in the classroom. But just as the guidelines themselves should be kept to a reasonable minimum, so must the notices. It is of little value to plaster the classroom with them, or to make them look menacing. Where possible, simple and often jokey little illustrations are of more value and more likely to capture attention than mere words.

Within this clear framework, the teacher then observes the following procedures:

- Children are set realistic standards and learning tasks.

- The teacher operates confidently, with a clear voice and without nervous mannerisms.

- The teacher gets to know the chidren in the class and to recognize the reasons behind their actions.

- In behaviour towards the children the teacher signals acceptance, support, and a belief in success.

- The teacher anticipates likely class control problems, decides on strategies for dealing with them and operates these strategies promptly and consistently.

- The children are given all reasonable opportunities for exercising democracy and responsibility.

- The children are presented with relevant and thus interesting learning tasks, and are allowed to experience success.

- The teacher uses change of activity within the lesson to avoid the class becoming bored and restless.

- The classroom environment is made as welcoming, colourful and stimulating as possible.

- The teacher avoids unnecessary or impractical threats.

- Clear directions are given to the class before any change of activity, and this change is carried out under carefully controlled conditions.

- Children are helped to see the consequences of their actions.

- The teacher recalls personal childhood classroom experience as a way of helping interpret the behaviours of the class.

Similarities and differences between the cognitive and the behavioural approaches

There is no necessary conflict between the behavioural approach, discussed in Chapter 4, and the cognitive approach to classroom control. Indeed they complement each other at a number of points, and overlap in a variety of ways. In both the behavioural and the cognitive approach teachers are prompted to look carefully at their own behaviours when problems of class control arise. Often unwittingly it is these very behaviours that have prompted the problems in the first place, and/or that serve to sustain them once they have occurred. In both approaches teachers are encouraged to observe children's behaviour equally carefully, in order to analyse that behaviour and relate it to the context in which it occurs. However, whereas the behaviourist focuses prime attention upon the reinforcement that such behaviour receives, the cognitive psychologist tries to tease out less obvious factors like motivation and interest, and to ascertain the way in which children conceptualize and make sense of the environment and of their own relationship to that environment.

But the reinforcement that children happen to receive for their actions is part of that environment, and therefore an important factor in determining the kind of sense they make of it. The cognitive psychologist is thus as interested in reinforcement as is the behaviourist. The difference arises in that the cognitive psychologist would advocate talking to the child and attempting, through discussion and debate, to change the child's behaviour even before alterations have been made in schedules of reinforcement. Many children respond quite happily and promptly to being talked to in this way, and a large number of control problems can be dealt with like this without resorting to the behavioural programmes discussed in Chapter 4.

The cognitive psychologist calls this debate and discussion *cognitive restructuring*, since the teacher helps the individual children concerned to restructure the way in which they think about and interpret their environment and themselves. Preferring a more direct terminology, the teacher simply calls it 'reasoning' with the child. But such reasoning is, of course, only likely to be successful if the teacher first gets to know the child well and to understand the child's problems and the causes underlying these problems. Where such reasoning fails, the cognitive psychologist would find a behaviour modification programme perfectly acceptable, though would suggest that most children see through the programme readily enough, and only decide to go along with it if they recognize it as bringing desirable results.

Rewards and punishments. In the area of rewards and punishments, there would be a wide measure of agreement between cognitivists and behaviourists. In fact the lengthy discussion of these factors in Chapter 4 applies equally well in this chapter, and there is no need to repeat it. But the cognitive psychologist would suggest in addition that many rewards are in fact *internal* to the child. However they may have come into being originally, these rewards now take the form of a sense of personal pleasure and satisfaction at a task well done, which feeds through into enhanced feelings of self-esteem and competence. Indeed the teacher should actively set out to encourage this internal reward system, and the self-motivation that goes with it, by helping children to reflect upon their successes and their achievements, and to conceptualize themselves during this reflection as people with increasing mastery over their environment and over the behaviours that are likely to bring them satisfaction in life. This applies not just (or even primarily) to academic work, but to social skills and to the ability to understand and guide one's own actions and the ideas and emotions that give rise to these actions. Children are therefore helped to internalize what I have called their locus of control, to gain confidence in their own abilities, to derive pride from taking responsibility for themselves, and to explore the benefits of working harmoniously with others both within school and outside school.

Objections to the cognitive approach

The main objections that can be levelled at the cognitive approach are:

> *It is vague and imprecise, since we cannot see what goes on inside the child's head.*

This is true of course. Nevertheless this criticism could be levelled at most aspects of our relationships with other people. We cannot see inside their heads, so we make assumptions about them on the basis of what they tell us and on what we can observe and find out about them. For the most part these assumptions work well enough for us to relate satisfactorily to our fellows. In the cognitive approach to classroom control, teachers are moreover prompted by such strategies as have been discussed in this chapter to develop their ability to understand and evaluate what the children in their class are about. The non-psychologist calls this being a good judge of people, and it one important element in the stock-in-trade of the successful teacher.

> *The cognitive approach is very subjective. Each teacher will develop his or her own exclusive cognitive maps, thus denying the children the consistency that is part of the behavioural approach.*

This is a danger, and draws attention to the need for a common policy throughout the school on matters of class control, and for frequent discussions amongst the staff on individual children and their circumstances and problems (see Chapter 6). Individual variations amongst teachers are bound to remain, and it would be misleading for the children if they did not, since one of the important lessons taught by the school is the diversity and variety of human nature, and the need to develop strategies for dealing with this diversity and variety. But by developing and operating a common policy in essential matters of class control the school provides the child with sufficient consistency for him or her to make sense of what is going on and to understand the values and standards that are being operated and the reasons behind them.

> *Changes in behaviour do not necessarily follow changes in attitude. Thus one may reason with children and they may honestly intend to change their ways in consequence, but often they will fail to do so.*

Again this is a danger. The behaviourist takes the view that instead of trying to change children's attitudes by cognitive restructuring, and then expecting them to change their behaviour to conform to these new attitudes, we should first change their behaviour and then allow the attitudes to change in their own time. That is, we should watch for examples of the wanted behaviour and quickly reinforce these, rather than wait for children to change their behaviour as a result of our having 'reasoned' them into a change of attitude. And doubtless on occasions the behaviourist is right. The fact that we help children to see the errors of their ways is no guarantee that they will now change them, just as helping a smoker to appreciate the dangers of smoking will not necessarily make him or her give up the habit. But, equally, on occasions the behaviourist is wrong. People do change their behaviour sometimes when they come to grasp how misguided or counter-productive that behaviour is. People *can* give up smoking as a result of reasoned argument. So talking to children clearly does lead to changes in behaviour. Indeed, if this were not the case, most of what the teacher does in the classroom would be a waste of time. The best technique is often therefore a combination of the cognitive approach and the behavioural approach. We help a child to accept the need for a change in behaviour, and then make sure that we catch the first signs of this change and reinforce it along behavioural lines. The child will then see concrete proof of the benefits to be gained from this new behaviour, and in consequence it will be more likely to become a permanent part of his or her repertoire.

Correctly applied, the cognitive approach need not, therefore, lead to the kinds of disadvantage suggested above. Its essence is that it helps children to reflect upon their own behaviour, to identify the various factors that act as influences upon them, to weigh the consequences of particular forms of behaviour, and to interpret more accurately the intentions that other people have towards them. Perhaps most important of all it helps them to modify and, as appropriate, develop their perception of themselves and the evaluations they place upon their own actions and upon their long and short-term goals. Ultimately, it is designed to transfer the controlling influences that operate upon their behaviour from other people to themselves. As they come to understand more clearly the issues that confront them within the classroom and in the outside world, so they become progressively more able to assume responsibility for their own actions and for formulating their own academic, social and ultimately vocational objectives. The lessons which they learn in self-control can therefore operate to grant them more freedom in the ordering of their lives rather than less. Conforming to the standards of behaviour expected by the teacher may at times seem irksome to children. But the more they are able to understand the reasons behind and the necessity for these standards, and the more they are able to feel that these standards are open to debate and to sensible modification by the class themselves, the more these standards will serve as an agent of education rather than simply as a convenient way for the teacher to keep the class in order.

References

On locus of control and attribution theory see respectively: Nisbett, R.E. and Ross, L.D. (1980) *Human Inference: Strategies and shortcomings of social judgement.* Englewood Cliffs: Prentice Hall.

Phares, E.J. (1973) *Locus of Control: A Personality Determinant of Behaviour.* Morriston, NJ: General Learning Press.

For a more general account of cognitive psychology see: Mayer, R.E. (1981) *The Promise of Cognitive Psychology.* San Francisco: W.H. Freeman.

Chapter 6

Strategies
III: Management Techniques

I have already drawn attention, particularly in Chapters 3 and 5, to the significance for class control of a school curriculum and of a lesson content that appears relevant to the children, and which is responsive to their particular needs and backgrounds. In Chapter 1 I discussed the variations between children in terms of ability levels, age/sex variables, and socio-economic variables, and stressed (and again in Chapters 4 and 5) the damaging effect upon children of a curriculum that exposes them to the experience of repeated personal failure. In the present chapter I link up these themes to the question of how to structure the day-to-day organization of the classroom so that it provides a satisfactory learning environment in which problems of class control are kept to a minimum.

Simple rules of classroom management

Whether working with very young children or with school leavers, the observation by teachers of certain straightforward rules of classroom management is a vital factor in the operation of good classroom control. By management, I mean the way in which individual teachers organize their approach to learning and organize the classroom as an aid to that learning.[1] Through good management, teachers are able to present themselves and the work to be undertaken in a manner likely to prompt in children the desirable cognitive maps discussed in Chapter 5. They are also able to carry out more effectively the observational and the reinforcement strategies discussed in Chapter 4.

Good management allows the children to get a clear picture of what is going on and what is expected of them, and allows them to see more clearly the consistent consequences of their own behaviour, both desirable and undesirable. It also allows teachers to think more clearly about their own work, to identify more accurately the successful and unsuccessful strategies in their teaching repertoire, and to make changes as they appear necessary. Instead of dissipating energies in the sheer labour of keeping on top of things, good class-room management in addition helps the teacher focus more clearly upon the task in hand, maintain a more accurate picture of what is going on in the classroom (the importance of such a picture was emphasized in Chapter 5), and develop a more positive and confident image of professional competence.

The basic 'rules' of good classroom management are as follows.

Be punctual. Many class control problems start because the teacher is either late arriving for the lesson, or is still involved in putting out apparatus and equipment when the children arrive. By starting the lesson on time, the teacher does not allow the opportunity for such problems to develop, and indicates to the class in addition personal efficiency and the importance of the work to be tackled. Punctuality at the end of the lesson is equally vital. Keeping children working after the bell and thus making them late for the next lesson only leads to ill-feeling, and the likelihood that the teacher's concluding remarks will be lost in the confusion as children start packing up and stampeding out of the room. It also seriously weakens the teacher's attempts to demand punctuality from the class. Equally bad is the habit of finishing too early, so leaving an awkward few minutes at the end of the lesson which the teacher tries desperately to fill and the children use for relieving frustrations that have built up during the lesson and for settling various private scores amongst themselves.

Be well prepared. This means not just in the major things, like the preparation of lesson material, but in the often overlooked minor things. An inadequate supply of pencils or of scissors for an essential task, a tape recorder or audio visual equipment that refuses to work or that has the wrong leads or connections, a shortage of chairs, visual aids that are too small for most of the children to see, a lack of coloured chalks or of felt pens for the overhead projector, glue pots that have gone hard or batteries that have gone dead, are all a direct invitation to merriment and teasing from the class. Like unpunctuality, they detract in the children's minds from a concept of the teacher as an efficient and effective manipulator of the learning environment.

Settle the class quickly to work. Once the teacher and the children are in the room, a quick and decisive start to the lesson is required, so that the children's attention is focused upon the teacher and upon the learning task. The lesson may begin with a few minutes of question-and-answer revision, with the presentation of a visual aid, or with any other relevant strategy, but the important consideration is that this strategy should immediately capture the attention of the class and get them involved. Often a practical activity during these opening minutes is better than a launch into unrelieved teacher talk. But whatever the strategy used, it should be designed to arouse interest, and prevent a long 'settling-down' episode, in which children are very much left to decide for themselves whether they want to start work or not.

Insist on full class co-operation. However good the opening strategy, there will always be occasions when some children are far too involved in their own conversations to be aware that the lesson has got underway. Or, for one reason or another, there may already be a babble of sound against which the teacher's attempt to introduce material, no matter how exciting it happens to be, is comprehensively lost. The rule here is to obtain full co-operation before starting work. It is of little use to try and out-shout the class, or to rely on those who are listening to shush the others. The teacher must have at his or her command an unfailing device for quietening the class and gaining attention. One such device, which was introduced in Chapter 5, is to call the name of an individual child or of individual children. Another is to clap the hands sharply (though practise this clandestinely at home, so that you can produce an effective sound at first go rather than a feeble slap which no one can be expected to take seriously!). Another is to tap the board rubber firmly on the desk. The first of these three devices is undoubtedly the best, but whichever one is used, the approach of the teacher must be firm, brisk and efficient. The children must be left in no doubt that the teacher means business.

Use the voice effectively. The voice is the teacher's main line of communication to the class. It is a medium through which children are helped to learn, and a medium through which the teacher exercises the majority of managerial functions. Obviously it should be used to communicate clearly and with sufficient volume. Used expressively, it can also add colour and interest to even relatively humdrum matters. It should be a voice which children find it pleasant to listen to, and a voice which the teacher can use all day without undue strain. To some teachers such a voice comes naturally, but to others a certain amount of practice is necessary. Such practice is time well spent.

A useful servant in this respect is the tape recorder. The teacher should tape record his or her voice when undertaking such activities as reading a passage of poetry or prose, speaking conversationally, giving instructions, and in action with the class. Playing back the tape and listening to it critically will indicate to the teacher where improvement is necessary. And practice in producing the voice by relaxing the muscles of the throat and larynx and producing the necessary energy from the diaphragm will considerably reduce the strain on the vocal chords.

Be alert to what is happening in the class. I have already made reference to the importance of this in Chapter 5. Good teachers give the class the impression they have eyes in the back of their heads. They move around the room, they use eye contact, and they accurately identify the areas where trouble is likely to start in the classroom and pay particular attention to them. But there is more to it from an organizational point of view even than this. Good teachers organize themselves so that they have the freedom to make decisions, so that they are able to decide for themselves where their presence is needed in the room and not have the children constantly decide the matter for them. A definite routine is essential here, with children well aware, for example, of the set procedures for asking for help, and with the teacher either ignoring or indicating firmly unavailability to children who choose to ignore these procedures.

Analyse what is happening in the class. Throughout the book I have emphasized the importance for the teacher of understanding the reasons behind children's behaviour, whether in terms of the reinforcement this behaviour is receiving or in terms of less tangible things like motivation, locus of control and self-concepts. From an organizational point of view, the teacher must retain scope for observing carefully what is going wrong and analysing the factors involved. A video tape of the lesson is obviously invaluable, but not a practical proposition for most teachers. However, in small group work a tape recorder can be useful, with the teacher playing the tape privately afterwards and listening particularly to his or her own performance. Was there an unnecessary edge to the voice when speaking to a particular child, a weariness when speaking to another, particular encouragement when talking to a third? Was there a hint of boredom on occasions, a 'talking down' to the children, a tendency to nag or to snap continually at a minor in-fringement? Does what was intended at the time to be a joke now sound rather unkind to the child concerned? And so on.

Analysis of this kind can greatly help teachers appreciate the kind of cognitive picture which the children are constructing of them, and upon which I laid great emphasis in Chapter 5. An alternative to the tape recorder is to have a colleague sit in on the lesson, and to use one of the interaction analysis instruments currently avail-able. With the use of this instrument, the colleague can keep a record of, for example, the number of times the teacher offers praise to children, or accepts their ideas, or directs questions at them. Many teachers are surprised when they study this record at the end of the lesson at how little they interacted with certain children, or at how infrequently they offered humour or supportive comments. Since colleagues can each sit in on each other's lessons, there is no reason why individuals should feel in any sense threatened by the presence of a fellow-teacher in the room.

Have clear and well-understood strategies for dealing with crises. Particularly in the primary school, there are frequent occasions when some minor crisis occurs which, for the rest of the class, adds enormous colour and dramatic opportunity to the lesson. Water or paint is spilled in an art lesson for example, a flower pot is knocked over and broken, a child is noisily and splashingly sick. Such events can easily be handled without a threat to class control if both teacher and children are well prepared and know exactly what is to be done. The whole incident is at once played down and coped with efficient-ly. Without needing to be told, one of the paint monitors fetches the floor cloth to deal with the spilt paint or water, another goes for the dustpan and brush and sheets of newspaper if there is broken glass for the teacher to deal with. The sick child is taken out to the cloak-room while another child goes for the caretaker (or for the mop and bucket if the teacher is to tackle the job of clearing up). Not only is the crisis quickly over, but the children are given yet further proof of the teacher's effectiveness at coping with whatever is likely to happen in the classroom.

Allocate teacher attention fairly. An analysis of classroom inter-ac of the type discussed above often indicates that teachers spend a disproportionate amount of their time with certain individ-uals or groups. The brighter children might be so favoured for example, while the less able are left to fend for themselves. Or it could just as easily be the other way around. The relatively ignored children, left to their own devices, may quickly serve as a focus for disruptive activities, with the teacher now interacting with them primarily to reprimand and punish. By allocating time fairly, the teacher is able to give individual children appropriate guidance and to help them feel that the teacher cares about their work and their progress.

Avoid drawing comparisons. It is good strategy, as I suggested in Chapter 4, for the teacher to draw attention to good work, particularly (from the class control point of view) if the child carries prestige and therefore serves as a role model for the others. But making comparisons, that is, telling some children that their performance is not up to the standard of others, is undesirable and can lead not only to hostility and resentment towards the teacher on the part of those who emerge adversely from such comparisons, but also to divisions within the class itself, with one group of children feeling that the teacher is making favourites out of another. Such resentment and such divisions are both likely to lead to unnecessary problems of class control.

Keep up-to-date with marking. Not only does work that is speedily marked and returned to children help them with their learning, it also helps the teacher to monitor progress and help with difficulties. From the class control point of view it helps in addition to provide the lesson with an important area of focus, and to maintain good relationships between teacher and class. The majority of children are anxious to get their work back and to see how they have fared, and appreciate a teacher who goes to some trouble to see it is returned promptly. Work should also be handed back with smiles and kind words, and should never under any circumstances be flung dramatically across the room. If teachers show themselves to have no respect for children's efforts or for the school property on which it is written, they can hardly expect such respect from the class.

Make sure promises are kept. I warned in Chapter 5 against uttering unrealistic threats which cannot be kept. The same is true of promises. If the teacher promises to help a child in some way, or to provide a treat of some kind for the class, then the promise should be a practical one and it should be kept. Failure to keep promises (usually greeted rightly with deep groans by the class) naturally produces resentment in children, and is hardly a useful incentive to them to keep their own promises to the teacher. If, as occasionally happens, a promise has to be broken for reasons outside the control of the teacher, then these reasons must be explained fully to the class and some form of compensatory action taken.

Make good use of questions. The teacher who poses frequent questions at the class, directing them at specific children, is using a valuable strategy for keeping everyone attentive and active. If a child is likely to be asked a question at any moment during the lesson, he or she has far more incentive to remain focused on the teacher than if allowed to chat in safety with a neighbour under the cover of the child in front, or dream up strategies for causing a disruption as soon as the occasion arises. Discussion of the skills associated with class questions lies outside the scope of this book, but the teacher should vary these questions, using some purely factual ones and others which are designed to make children think creatively, or to tease out the relationships between the various pieces of information that they have just been given. The introduction of variety into teacher questions maintains interest and again helps to focus attention on the teacher.

Ensure adequate opportunities for practical activities. As was seen in Chapter 1, it is a rough rule of thumb that the 'teacher talk' part of a lesson should occupy no more than a minute to a minute and a half (dependent upon the ability of the class) for each year of the children's age. Thus a class of bright 10-year-olds might be expected to listen to the teacher for perhaps 15 minutes, before becoming restless. If the teacher's material is uninteresting, or if there is failure on the teacher's part to pose sufficient class questions or to respond to the children's attempts to ask questions, then this restlessness will start much earlier. Note that, as in Chapter 1, I am not saying that the teacher should talk for this length of time, simply that to go on much longer will be to invite problems of class control. Once this period (or a lesser one) is up, the children should be offered the opportunity for practical work. Children, both at primary and secondary level, enjoy doing things, rather than being expected to sit and listen. So the great majority of lessons should include their practical component if the control problems associated with restlessness and boredom are to be avoided. Remember that 'practical activities' do not simply mean ambitious things with chemicals or paints. Writing, reading, working at exercises, drawing a diagram are all practical activities. An important rule that holds good in all cases is that the teacher must have prepared the work carefully so that it runs smoothly, and that ample time is allowed for the change over from one activity to another and for any clearing up that is required afterwards. Also essential are the clear cognitive guidelines to which I made reference in Chapter 5.

Wherever practical, delegate routine classroom tasks to the children. Children, particularly of primary school age but in the secondary school as well, like to have jobs around the classroom for which they are responsible. It indicates the teacher's trust in them, their own place as significant members of the class, and the fact that the classroom is their concern as well as that of the teacher. In addition, by having the children attend to routine chores the teacher is able to ensure the smooth running of the classroom and to have time to tackle other essential tasks. By insisting that all children are given their fair turn at these chores the teacher is also able to give some of the more troublesome children the experience of responsibility. An added bonus is that while these latter children are helping out during break or after school, the teacher now has the chance for the informal and relaxed chats with them that are essential if they are to be understood as people. These chats also help the teacher detect the presence of those factors in the children's backgrounds which, as I discussed in Chapters 1 and 2, contribute towards unwanted classroom behaviours.

Organize the classroom effectively. In the primary school, where the teacher usually remains in the same room with the class most of the day, it is rather easier to see that the seating and the various items of classroom equipment are appropriately positioned. In the secondary school, where the teacher may move from classroom to classroom, this often means visiting the room before the lesson begins and checking up on how it is arranged and whether or not everything is to hand. I talked in Chapter 3 about the importance of a conveniently ordered classroom if many of the situations likely to lead to difficulties of control are to be avoided. A little extra time and thought devoted to creating this order pay enormous dividends, as does the readiness to alter things to meet changing circumstances. It is all too easy for a teacher, even during the space of a single school year, to become set in his or her ways, and to insist that children conform to these ways, instead of studying what is actually needed and making the necessary adjustments to accommodate the environment to it.

Deal with children's problems. There are few things more frustrating for a child at school than to have a problem which he or she tries in vain to draw to the attention of the teacher. To the child the problem is an important one, to the teacher it apparently matters little if at all. The child may never have been issued with a textbook for example, and may continually be called upon to share because the teacher lacks the time to go to the stock cupboard at the other end of the school building; or the child may have parents who are unwilling or unable to buy required items of school clothing or equipment. Or the child may have missed some vital work through absence. Or be sitting too far from the board, or with unfriendly children. Or be having difficulties with another member of staff. Or have had something stolen by another child. Or be unable to understand some groundwork gone through at the beginning of term, and be experiencing trouble in understanding what is now being covered. Or have problems at home or as a result of bullying by other children.

The list is endless, but in each case the child is experiencing an anxiety which the teacher is apparently too busy to heed. Good classroom organization always allows the teacher both a time and a place to listen to this anxiety. The children are left in no doubt that the teacher has a friendly, informal but nevertheless clear routine for listening to their individual problems. It may be during break or after school. If the classroom is busy at such times, then there will be another room to which teacher and child can repair. It may be the deputy head's room or the year tutor's room, but it will be somewhere where uninterrupted talk can take place, and the child will be sure of confidentiality.

Similarly, good class management should allow opportunities for the airing of whole-class problems. Perhaps part of a lesson will be set aside regularly for a 'review' of work so far, and for the children to give their reactions in a friendly and non-judgemental atmosphere. And the children will be left in no doubt that their views are respected, that democracy will be allowed to operate where possible, and that where action can be taken to put things right the teacher will be willing and able to undertake it.

Conclude the lesson successfully. In addition to concluding the lesson promptly, having allowed ample time for clearing away and for any work or instructions that need to be given to the children, it is important that the teacher parts from the class on a friendly note.

Such advice may sound to be asking the impossible if the children's conduct has been the very opposite of endearing, but it makes the task of facing them again that much easier. And for the primary school teacher, the next encounter could be only 15 minutes away at the end of break. A genial leave-taking has the added advantage of indicating to the children that whatever has gone wrong during the lesson has failed to leave the teacher in the least bit upset, a useful way of showing the troublemakers how ineffectual their behaviour has been. Of course if the lesson, like the great majority of lessons, has gone well, then the teacher should praise the class for their good work, and show clearly that he or she is looking forward to meeting them next time. Finally, if the class are to leave the room, they should be dismissed in an orderly fashion (which again conveys a favourable impression for them to carry over to the next lesson), row by row if necessary and with everyone waiting their turn orderly and quietly.

Planning the lesson

Although I have stressed the great importance for class control of a curriculum and a lesson content which are relevant to the children's needs, geared correctly to their levels of ability, and presented in a stimulating fashion, a detailed discussion of teaching method lies outside this book's scope. Nevertheless, the way in which lessons are planned and organized has considerable bearing upon class control. Clearly, ill-prepared work which leaves the teacher floundering for material before the lesson is half over is inviting control problems. So is a lesson that contains too much material, with the teacher struggling to get through, the class confused and frustrated at hurried attempts to explain difficult areas, and work regularly left half-finished when the bell goes. So is a lesson which contains insufficient practical work, the importance of which I have emphasized several times, or a lesson which allows children insufficient scope to express and develop their own particular areas of interest within the subject concerned. Needless to say, however the lesson is planned, the teacher who does not know his or her teaching subject or who fails to keep up-to-date and who in spite of frantic attempts of covering-up has his or her ignorance exposed time and time again by the class, is hardly likely to command respect or cooperation.

Precision teaching. One valuable approach to organizing and planning the lesson, and one which helps place the teacher in a position where class control becomes a less likely problem, is what is known as *precision teaching.* Precision teaching takes its start from what it claims are the five key teaching questions:

- Is the pupil on the right task (in terms of abilities and interests)?
- Is the pupil learning?
- Is the pupil learning quickly enough (particularly important if there is lost ground to be made up)?
- What should be done if the pupil is not learning or not learning quickly enough?
- What level of performance should be expected?

In order to provide appropriate answers to these questions, precision teaching suggests that when planning and teaching a lesson the teacher must:

1. *Specify in advance the desired pupil performance in observable, measurable terms.* This involves the formulation of lesson objectives which express clearly the child behaviours that should be apparent at the end of the lesson if this has been a success. Since learning implies a *change* in behaviour, all that the teacher is being asked to do here is to say what kind of a change it is intended to bring about in children as a result of the lesson that is to be taught.

2. *Record pupil performance regularly and systematically.* Record keeping is far too big a topic to go into here, but the use of frequent brief *assessment probes* (written or oral revision questions which the children are asked to answer) with the results noted down by the teacher, is invaluable. The word 'probe' is used rather than test, since it is vital to get away from the notion that the children are being *judged* in any negative way. The purpose behind the probe is simply to help the teacher identify what has been learnt and what requires rather more practice, and the probe should be presented to the class in this light and in an informal and unstressful way.

3. *Record the teaching arrangements in relation to the performance.* Too often teachers fail to keep note of the methods and techniques they were using when children produced particular levels of assessed progress. Thus it becomes difficult in retrospect to link successful pupil work with the form of teaching which helped produce it. This makes it hard for teachers to evaluate their own performance, and hard to plan effectively how best to help individual children.

4. *Analyse the data regularly to see what changes are necessary.* This is not easy, since teachers are busy people, and once a particular scheme of lessons has been prepared, the natural temptation is to go on using it on subsequent occasions, or at best

only to make minor changes. But an examination of the data recorded as specified in 2 and 3 above often shows up inadequacies in what is being done, and may indicate clear opportunities for improvement. Children vary from one class to the next, and even within the same class changes are taking place all the time. For a primary school child in particular, a year sees a marked physical and psychological development. The teacher must be sensitive to this develoment, and must adapt teaching methods accordingly.

All the various points summarized above have been introduced elsewhere in this book, but it is convenient to draw them together here. Teachers who are not methodical in their approach to lesson planning, assessment, and record keeping make life hard both for themselves and for the class. Although at first things may seem to go well, the teacher's clear lack of organization, together with the omissions and the repetitions to which this lack of organization gives rise, are likely to encourage problems of class control before long. Add to this the children's inevitable recognition of the fact that the teacher has little real idea of their individual progress, and we have a recipe for turning these problems into major difficulties.

Structures of authority and support within the school

I indicated in Chapters 1 and 3 the importance for child behaviour of the way in which a school is structured and organized, and of the policies and practices which it operates. Little further need be added, except to stress again that from the class control point of view it is essential that the school is organized in such a way that:

- it is responsive to the needs of the children
- has clear and correctly understood lines of communication linking together all members of the school community
- keeps rules and regulations to a sensible minimum and makes sure that they are known, appreciated and observed by everyone
- indicates that the main purpose of the school is to help solve rather than create problems.

Closely linked to these organizational aims in terms of importance is the relevant and practical curriculum to which I referred in Chapters 3 and 5, a curriculum that is sensitive to all levels of ability and all backgrounds found within the school and that prepares children for the challenges and demands which they will have to face in real life. Equally closely linked to them is the provision within the school of an effective system of guidance, counselling and pastoral care. By this I mean a system that encourages and provides ample opportunity for children to discuss their problems with a sympathetic member of staff, who will not only listen but will have the necessary expertise to provide appropriate help.

Guidance, counselling and pupil care. The techniques of guidance, counselling and pastoral care lie outside the scope of this book but the essential aspect of them is that the child should be helped, in a friendly and non-judgemental atmosphere, to identify the real nature of his or her problems and to formulate solutions that are appropriate and practical for the particular circumstances in which he or she has to live life. The help must come from an individual whom the child can trust, who is a patient listener, who knows how to refrain from jumping in with ready-made 'solutions' which sound good in theory but which are unworkable for the child concerned, who is sensitive to the need for confidentiality, and who is prepared to take action on the child's behalf where such action is necessary.

As I indicated in Chapter 5, many class control problems come from children who feel themselves to be caught up in a system which they do not understand and which fails to understand them. Bored, frustrated and defensive, they see school simply as yet another source of difficulty in what is already a difficult enough life. Teachers are perceived as instigators of punishment rather than as instigators of support, and there appears to be no one on the staff who is attempting to see them as fellow human beings rather than simply as nuisances. This picture is usually unfair to the school, but nevertheless it is the picture that some children formulate. And if in addition they lack the language skills to communicate their problems to teachers in a form which the latter can readily understand, there is often little likelihood that they will be given the information that will enable them to redraw it.

The counselling and guidance network. The presence of an established guidance and counselling network, stretching from the class teacher to the deputy head and the headteacher, and embracing in addition at secondary school level the heads of year and perhaps the heads of department, is a necessity if children are to avoid misconceptions of this kind. Teachers themselves need to be conscious of the importance of this network, and to be committed to its use, while children should fully understand the procedures involved and should be given ample proof, when they resort to these procedures, of their value and their effectiveness.

This can only happen if the school, led by the example of the headteacher, sees itself as a *guidance community*, interested above all in helping children come to terms with themselves and with the social and vocational demands that living in the modern world will lay upon them. To make this community work, staff need regular meetings, usually in small, relevant groups, to discuss individual children and what the school is doing and can do to help them. This 'case conference' approach provides for a pool of information about children who are having difficulties of classroom behaviour and of other kinds, and allows for the development of common coping and helping strategies. As Chapter 8 will stress, it is also of great help to the teachers themselves, since it removes the sense of isolation and of struggling along without help from one's colleagues from which many teachers suffer.

But the case conference approach can only work well if it is built into the school's structure. It is of only limited value if it is restricted simply to trying to arrange a get-together of those involved on an *ad hoc* basis in the corner of the staff room during morning break. As intimated above, it is essential that the headteacher provides the right example here, and has the support and co-operation of the school's middle management and ultimately of each member of the teaching staff. The whole guidance and counselling network, in fact, should be seen as something in which everyone is involved and as something in which everyone has a democratic voice. In this way it will be sensitive to the abilities and perceptions of each member of staff, and each member of staff will therefore have a personal interest in making it work.

References

Interaction analysis can be followed up in: Delamont, S. (1983) (2nd edn) *Interaction in the Classroom*. London: Methuen.

For precision teaching see: Formentin, T. and Csapo, M. (1980) *Precision Teaching*. Vancouver: Centre for Human Development and Research.

For guidance and counselling see: Nelson-Jones, R. (1983) *Practical Counselling Skills*. London: Holt, Rinehart and Winston.

Chapter 7

Teacher Behaviours and Classroom Control

I have been discussing teacher behaviours throughout the book, but it is time now to say a little more about the specific qualities in the teacher which seem to go with good classroom control, and about the coping strategies which he or she can use when faced with particular emergencies or with particular threats to classroom order. Let me take the matter of teacher qualities first.

Teacher qualities and classroom control

In spite of the research that has been carried out over the years in both the USA and the UK on the characteristics of the successful teacher, we still have surprisingly little hard data. So much depends upon factors external to the teacher, such as the age and ability and socio-economic backgrounds of the children, the subject being taught, the environment provided by the school, and the range of other variables which have been discussed throughout the book. What works for one teacher in one set of circumstances, therefore, may very well not work for another teacher or for the same teacher in other circumstances. Nevertheless, there are certain important qualities about which we can generalize. External matters, such as voice and mannerisms have already been dealt with (Chapters 3 and 5), as have such considerations as the ability to interest and stimulate, the ability to plan and organize, the ability to understand children, and the ability to know clearly what is going on at any time in the classroom (Chapters 3, 4, 5 and 6). My concern now, therefore, is more with matters of temperament and personality, in other words with the affective side of the teacher's life, and the teacher's personal belief systems and standards.

Fairness and a sense of humour. When asked to rate the qualities in teachers which they admire, children of all ages put *fairness* at or near the head of their lists. I made reference to fairness when discussing the importance of consistency in Chapter 5. To a child, fairness in a teacher means that the teacher adopts a uniform set of standards and procedures when relating to the class, so that the class is able to identify clearly what is required of them and what kinds of behaviour are acceptable and unacceptable. To this could be added that the fair teacher is one who cares enough about children to see to it that everyone is given equal opportunities and equal help and support.

Close to fairness in importance in the minds of children is a *sense of humour*. They respond well to a teacher who can share a joke with the class, and particularly to a teacher who can see the funny side even when the laugh is on him or her. A humorous teacher is, therefore, a person who not only has the ability to amuse others, but is also ready to be amused by them. This emphatically does not mean laughing at children, or using them as butts for jokes, simply that the children as well as the teacher are allowed opportunities to initiate the laughter from time to time, with the teacher joining in along with everyone else. Shared humour of this kind reduces the barriers between teacher and class, and provided that it is not overdone helps the class to see the teacher as an ally and friend rather than as a member of an opposing species. And children are much more likely to co-operate with allies and friends than with opponents, thus reducing the number of incidents that can lead to class control problems.

Relaxation, self-control and patience. Another advantage of laughing with the class as the occasion presents itself is that this shows the class not only that the teacher is a human being but is a relaxed and confident one at that. A teacher who stands too much on dignity, or who is habitually cold and remote, may in fact be fearful of what might happen if the defences were lowered at all. Which brings me to my next point, namely that the teacher who is by nature *calm and relaxed* is much less likely to become angry when faced by a control problem. Anger, particularly when it goes with an outright loss of temper, may well make the teacher over-react to a piece of misbehaviour, thus perhaps angering the child in turn and making a bad situation even worse. It is in addition often difficult to act objectively when in a temper, thus opening the way amongst other things to the kind of wild threats against which I warned in Chapter 5. Clearly a teacher who is unable to practise self-control is hardly in an ideal position to demand such self-control from the class, or to face them easily again after cooling down. Certainly there may be occasions when the teacher will want to speak sharply to the class or to individuals in order to add emphasis to what is being said, but this is a very different matter from an actual loss of temper. A calm and relaxed manner, which remains unruffled in the face of whatever kind of classroom crisis happens to occur, is a highly effective attribute in all areas of a teacher's task, and perhaps most particularly in the area of class control.

Linked in turn to a calm and relaxed manner is the value of *patience*. The teacher who is patient in the face of children's learning difficulties is far more likely to remain relaxed and far less likely to discourage, frighten or antagonize children than is the teacher who finds these difficulties a continual source of frustration. Some people appear by nature to have a readier store of patience than others, but in a teacher patience depends to a considerable extent upon realistic expectations of what levels of performance children can produce (see Chapter 5). If the teacher has an arbitrary set of standards, unrelated to the children's abilities or to their previous learning experiences, then he or she is going to find slow progress a constant irritation, and is likely to perceive the children concerned in a very negative light, even to the extent of thinking this slowness is deliberate. The truth of the matter is that very few people prefer to fail than to succeed. Children in the main will learn if they can. If work is proving difficult for them, this is initially at least usually because they cannot understand the concepts or the skills involved. The patient teacher therefore regards the child's 'slowness' as useful feedback, and re-presents the learning material in a more appropriate form, ensuring that as often as possible the child is given the opportunity to experience success (Chapters 2 and 5). This experience of success allows the child to remain motivated, to make the necessary effort at comprehension. As learning takes place, the teacher in turn experiences success, and is able to see him or herself as making a real professional contribution to the child's life – one of the most rewarding aspects of the teacher's job.

Explaining things appropriately and having time for children. It is also easier to remain patient if the teacher has the ability to explain things to children in a form which they can understand. Class control problems can occur on occasions not because the teacher's lesson material is intrinsically uninteresting or not related to the children's needs, but because he or she is unable to convey it to them in a suitable way. The children are thus prevented from constructing the cognitive map of the subject which I talked about in Chapter 5, and become bored and restless. Putting material across in a suitable way (often referred to by teachers as 'getting down to the children's level') depends to an important degree upon understanding the children's stage of cognitive develoment, as was seen in Chapter 5. But it also depends upon being genuinely interested in the children's world, in the things which can be presented to them as appropriate examples, in the analogies which are likely to make sense to them and capture their imagination, in the anecdotes and brief digressions which are likely to refocus attention on the teacher if it shows signs of waning, in the hobbies which the children have, the books which they read and the television programmes they enjoy, and in the attitudes and opinions which they hold. Generally, the teacher who is interested in the child's world and who has this kind of knowledge is the teacher who is prepared to spend time talking to children and in actually listening to what they have to say. This applies not just to lesson time, but to appropriate moments during break and lunchtime and after school. I am talking here not simply about extra-curricular activities such as sports clubs and school societies (though these are vital), but to those occasions when the teacher has a group of children voluntarily staying behind to help with classroom jobs or with some project that has captured everyone's interests.

This brings me neatly to my next point, which is that the successful teacher is someone who always seems to *have time for children*. Children are helped to feel that their affairs matter enough for the teacher to want to attend to them, or to arrange a more convenient time when the child can return if the present moment is out of the question. Thus a good positive relationship is formed between the teacher and the child, which carries over directly into matters of class control. The child perceives the teacher as someone who is ready to help, and the child is then motivated to help the teacher by classroom co-operation in return. There are always the exceptions of course, the children who seem unwilling to accept help or to be ungrateful when it is forthcoming. But frequently this is because what the teacher perceives as help is not thus perceived by the child (see Chapter 5). Or it may be that help is offered exclusively on the teacher's terms, rather than as part of a kind of informal, unwritten performance contract (Chapter 4), with both teacher and child tacitly or explicitly agreeing to give and take. Either way, the child decides that the help is of little value to him or her and in consequence fails to see gratitude as entering into the matter.

Investing in good classroom control. To the teacher who claims that none of the qualities mentioned in this chapter come naturally and who fails to see the point of acquiring any of them, the answer must be that I am talking essentially about an investment in the cause of good class control. However hard it may at first sight seem to acquire things like calmness and patience, it is even harder to have to battle day in and day out with problem groups of children. Like most other things, if teaching is worth doing it is worth doing well. And if it is done well, it is the teacher, not just the children, who reaps the benefits. Unless the teacher recognizes he or she is in the wrong profession (in which case there is little point in remaining) then time and effort spent acquiring the skills of the trade, in terms of personality as well as in terms of other behaviours, is probably the best professional investment that the teacher is likely to make.

Coping strategies for particular threats to classroom control

I now turn to an examination of particular incidents which may pose a sharp, immediate threat to the teacher's control of the class. In dealing with these incidents the teacher will be using the principles which underlie all the strategies that I have been discussing so far in this book.

Let me make a survey of them and indicate how the teacher might best use a knowledge of these principles to respond to them.

Rudeness. Every teacher is all too familiar with those occasions when a child reacts with seeming insolence to something the teacher says. This insolence can take the form of a verbal remark, or a display of what many teachers (for want of a better term) refer to as 'dumb insolence'; the child casts eyes heavenwards, or sighs deeply, or looks contemptuously at the teacher, or walks away while the teacher is talking, or contrives somehow to do a combination of these things at once. What should the teacher do? Firstly, and emphatically, the experience should not be allowed to provoke anger. As I said earlier in the chapter, anger lessens the teacher's scope for acting objectively. It also indicates to the child, more clearly than words, that the child's actions have struck home. The teacher is hurt by them, which is often exactly what the child wants. The anger is therefore a form of reinforcement to the child (see Chapter 4), and perhaps to other children looking on. At a cognitive level (Chapter 5), it indicates that the way to get your own back on the teacher is by being rude; and any subsequent punishment that the teacher hands out may well be worth it simply for the gratification of seeing him or her goaded into a display of temper.

Keeping one's temper on such occasions may not be easy, and I return in Chapter 8 to some of the issues involved in doing so. But having kept it, the teacher is now able to decide calmly on what action to take. This brings me to the second point, namely that whatever action is taken should be seen to be swift and decisive. Hesitation on the teacher's part, while he or she desperately hunts for ideas on what to do, is again potentially reinforcing for the child. Even if the rudeness did not make the teacher angry, it clearly was effective in nonplussing him or her. Thus the teacher must take note of the old Scout motto, and be prepared. Or take note of the question asked by some Zen Buddhists, 'Are you ready?', a question which relates to each experience that we meet in life. If we are unready, then we are constantly being disconcerted and confused by what happens to us, deciding only when it is too late what we should have said or done at the time. Naturally we cannot be ready for every event in detail, but we should have an attitude of mind that accepts the possibilities of whatever lies in store. Thus the teacher, knowing that rudeness is an all too common factor of school life, must have an attitude of mind that allows a prompt and firm response, without an agonizing pause each time while the brains are cudgelled for some clue as to how best to react.

In an important sense, the *decisiveness* of the response is part of the response itself. If the teacher remains calm and responds decisively, then he or she is indicating clearly to the child that the rudeness has had no effect. Nothing the child can do in that direction is relevant or powerful enough to hurt the teacher in any way at all. In a way calmness and decisiveness matter more than the actual details of whatever it is the teacher decides to do. Which brings me to the third point. The teacher may decide to ignore the child's remark or the dumb insolence, in the manner discussed in Chapter 4. Without indicating that he or she has even bothered to listen to or notice the child, the teacher turns away and carries on with the lesson. If on the other hand it is decided that intervention is necessary, then the teacher replies directly to the child, but makes sure that the reply is brief and to the point, and is emphatically not an invitation to the child to enter into a long dialogue of accusation and counter-accusation. If the teacher feels that the child's behaviour warrants further discussion, the child will brusquely be told, without reference to the reason (and thus without drawing every-one's attention further to the unwanted behaviour) to stay behind and see the teacher when the lesson is over. The work of the class is then promptly resumed. This swift action usually prevents the child from attempting to attract further attention by demanding to know the reason why instructions have been given to stay behind.

There will always be a minority of children, however, well-versed in the art of attention seeking and of annoying the teacher, who will manage to insert this demand whatever the teacher does, and will go on repeating it and disturbing the lesson until the teacher takes some notice. The temptation on the part of the teacher is now to try some rudeness back ('I should have thought that even you, Higgins, would have known the answer to that question!') or some sarcasm ('Yes, of course, it was silly of me to expect that you would be able to see what was wrong!'). Both temptations must be avoided. It is hardly sensible or productive policy to take a child to task for rudeness and then to be seen by all and sundry to be employing rudeness oneself. Sarcasm is just as bad, as it implies an insult to the person concerned. And both strategies only invite further rudeness in response, as the child involved now tries to reassert status in front of the rest of the class, or to revenge the wound which perhaps the teacher's words have inflicted. The correct response is to tell the child 'If you think, you'll know the answer to that question', thus indicating that the question was an unnecessary one, that the onus is now on the child, but that you do not doubt his or her ability to come up with the answer. The child is therefore not directly attacked in any way by the teacher's comment, and is in consequence not stung into the need for a reply. Indeed, if a reply is given, the child is now publicly casting doubt on his or her own competence to solve a question whose answer is readily apparent to everyone else in the class.

Note that the teacher does not mention the word 'rudeness' at all, which would be a way of clearly admitting a recognition of the force behind the child's behaviour. Even if it should be decided that this behaviour is not serious enough to warrant bothering with the child after the end of the lesson, the word 'rudeness' will still be avoided. A quick comment such as 'That was a silly remark, and if you'd thought more carefully you wouldn't have made it', is all that is required. The second part of this comment, which indicates the teacher's confidence in the child's powers of thinking, is as import-ant as the first. The rebuke contained in the opening words is followed up by an implied compliment, leaving the child again without any need for further rudeness in order to strike back at the teacher. Once again, further rudeness would indeed appear to demonstrate to the class the the child lacks the powers of thought which have just been attributed to him or her.

Where individual chidren are asked to stay behind, either in connection with rudeness or any other misdemeanour, it is counterproductive to turn on them angrily when they do so and demand an explanation of their behaviour during the lesson ('Now what have you got to say for yourself?'). The child will either remain stubbornly silent, no matter how much the teacher may persist with demands and with threats of dire punishment, or will enter into defensive denials or renewed rudeness. A far more effective strategy is to turn to the child when the room has emptied of the rest of the class and give a pleasant smile. The smile disarms the child (busily preparing mentally for the anticipated confrontation), who is left slightly disconcerted and therefore much more open to teacher influence. It also reinforces the impression of equanimity which the teacher gave when the rudeness actually occurred. And most important of all, it indicates to the child that the teacher has no intention of seeing their relationship in terms of mutual hostility. There is a much better way available, namely that of friendship and co-operation, and the teacher is always ready to try this way.

Having established this atmosphere, the teacher says words to the effect that 'You know perfectly well that wasn't a very sensible way of behaving, so I don't think we need go into any of the details need we?'. The child may simply agree, and further agree to the teacher's suggestion that behaviour will be more appropriate next time, and the matter can then be left to rest there. Rather than terminating the interview immediately, however, it is good policy for the teacher to reinforce the value of the more friendly relationship that has just been established by changing the subject and asking the child some questions about an area (perhaps a sport or a hobby or an extra-curricular or curricular activity) in which he or she is known to have competence. A remark such as 'Mrs Smith was telling me the other day how helpful you were with ...' or '... how good you are at ...?' or '... how interested you are in ...?' is an invaluable one. It shows the child that the teacher takes a sufficient interest to want to discuss successes with other teachers, and is obviously happy to retain this interest (a potential source of reinforcement to the child) in the future. It also, in a gentle but clear way, introduces an unspoken threat to a continuance of the child's good relationship with Mrs Smith. After all, a teacher who listens to the child's good points from Mrs Smith, will quite probably relay to her in turn the child's bad points should these persist in the future.

If the child's rudeness is habitual, and if the above strategy has been tried a number of times and seen not to work, then clearly the problem is one that goes beyond a single class teacher and becomes a whole school one. It is, therefore, time for the case study approach mentioned in Chapter 6, and for a common policy to be worked out for relating to the child. There is nothing to be gained by a teacher struggling on with a particularly difficult child when clearly colleagues are experiencing the same difficulties. A pooling of information, a sharing of those strategies which may have been found to work by some colleagues, and a common approach to the child in the future are all essential, with the headteacher and the school's middle management all closely involved.

Finally the reader must be reminded again of the points made in Chapters 1 and 2. If we wish to respond appropriately to a child's behaviour, we must try to understand what prompts this behaviour, which means taking into account the great range of individual differences between children. Thus what may be intended as rudeness by one child, may be seen as no more than thoughtlessness or high spirits if it comes from another. Children, especially young children, are often impetuous, and often unaware of the particular niceties of speech and behaviour expected by individual teachers. Clearly, the teacher cannot be seen to punish behaviour if it comes from one child and condone it in another, even though he or she may realize that the latter child does not intend to offend. But the quiet words that are exchanged with the children concerned after the lesson will differ. The former child knows perfectly well the nature of the transgression, and will be dealt with as indicated above. The second child will need friendly guidance as to what is expected in future, and a clear indication that the teacher fully appreciates that before receiving this guidance the child was in no position to understand that the behaviour being offered was inappropriate. He or she will also be left in no doubt that the teacher is there to help, and will continue to supply the necessary guidance in the future.

Defiance. By defiance I mean those moments perhaps dreaded most of all by the teacher, when a child is instructed to do something or other and point-blank refuses. Immediately an aghast, anticipatory hush descends upon the class. One of their number has issued what amounts to a direct challenge to the teacher's authority. How will the latter react? What will happen to the child? Will the teacher have a way of enforcing authority, or will there be a humiliating climb down? The teacher senses, quite rightly, that a great deal is at stake here. Failure to deal appropriately with the defiance will seriously weaken standing with the class. Yet how can a child, particularly a child in a large secondary school, be *made* to do something in such circumstances? The child's prestige is also at stake in front of the class. A climb down for him or her is likely to be in its way as humiliating as it would be for the teacher.

The first point to make is that the wise teacher appears to have a knack of avoiding incidents of this kind. In a way schoolteaching is, like politics, the art of the possible. There is no point in demanding something from an individual or individuals if it is clear that they will stubbornly refuse to deliver, no matter what is done or threatened. The wise teacher will not, therefore, make unrealistic demands. Children will not be asked to produce work in an absurdly short space of time or up to an unattainable standard. A child who is having a fit of the sulks, possibly as a result of something or other that happened at home that morning or in another lesson, will not be forced to participate in some unwelcome activity, such as reading aloud or answering class questions or coming out to write on the blackboard. Where the work is unavoidable, as in the case, for example, of a written exercise which the whole class is being asked to undertake, the moody child will simply be told, as the teacher passes by and glances at unattempted work, that there will be a lot to catch up on next time. Then as the class is leaving the room at the end of the lesson, or as the class pauses between one lesson and the next, the teacher will take the child to one side and say it is clear something is bothering him or her, and would they like to discuss it. If the answer is 'no' the teacher does not probe further, but in a matter-of-fact way remarks that everyone feels a little down at times, and hopefully the feeling will soon pass. In the meanwhile, there is some work to catch up on, and the child will be seen at a convenient time to discuss how this can be done.

Again, realism dictates that particularly difficult children are not asked, at least publicly, to carry out a classroom chore to which it is obvious they will make objection. Usually there is no shortage of willing volunteers, and such volunteers should always be called upon rather than trying to press reluctant individuals into service. However, it should be made tacitly clear to such individuals that their help is welcome should they wish to offer it.

Thus by knowing their children and proceeding sensibly, wise teachers are rarely faced with deliberate defiance. If it does occur, however, the initial rules are as those for rudeness. The teacher does not become angry, and acts decisively and calmly. If the child is at primary school level, simply taking him or her firmly (but not painfully) by the arm and leading them back to their place or wherever they have been asked to go is often quite sufficient. If the defiance persists, then the child is taken again equally firmly and led out to the headteacher's room. Where a child is this difficult, the headteacher will already have been apprised of the problem, and will have a strategy for coping. Often this strategy will take the form of a 'time-out' (see Chapter 4), with the child having to remain quietly in the headteacher's room until the latter deems it appropriate to return him or her to the class.

With older children, where physical interaction is for obvious reasons not recommended, a different approach is called for. Without raising the voice the teacher simply repeats the request, politely enough, and this time the child (who was perhaps hoping for a confrontation) now decides to give up and comply. If the latter again refuses, the teacher asks the reason. Just possibly, this may contain some justification, in which case the teacher acknowledges the fact, indicates that hitherto he or she was unaware of it, and leaves it at that. No one has lost face, and the teacher has demonstrated a capacity for reasonableness to the class. On the other hand, if the child has no acceptable justification, the teacher then says 'Yes, well I can see you don't want to do (whatever was asked). We all feel like that sometimes. I know I do. But it is important and that's why I would like you to do it.' The child is now able to comply without any loss of face, and having had his or her say may be ready to co-operate. At the same time, the child will recognize that the teacher has left the door open for co-operation, and may well feel grateful. No one has become angry, and no one has staked any prestige on the issue.

However, if the child still refuses, perhaps adding rudeness to the refusal, the teacher now has two choices open. The first is a simple shrug of the shoulders, and the child is told OK, but in that case they must come and see the teacher at the end of the lesson. This is not a strategy of defeat. The teacher has been careful not to invest full authority in the incident. There has been no 'Now do as you're told *at once*' or 'I'm giving you one last chance' or 'I'm *warning* you, Biggins'. Instead, there has been (as the rest of the class will have registered) a perfectly reasonable request and a perfectly reasonable attitude on the teacher's part. If the child decides not to respond, then clearly the teacher has no intention of wasting any further time on the matter, and will see the child about it individually later.

The second choice is for a direct confrontation with the child. The teacher is now staking a great deal on obtaining obedience, and if he or she goes this far, then victory must be secured. There is no question about that. Failure at this point would lead to the damage in authority to which I earlier drew attention. Again, however, it is inadvisable to offer a stern 'warning' of unspecified retribution. The teacher simply spells out the consequences of continued disobedience, namely that the child will have to see the headteacher (or whichever member of staff is responsible for such situations). Note that the teacher does not say the child will be 'sent' to the headteacher, since the child may doggedly refuse to go, necessitating a change of tactics on the part of the teacher. Instead, the child is told he or she will have to 'see' the headteacher. If there is another refusal, then it is left to the teacher to decide whether the child will respond to a direct instruction to go to the head's room (or to accompany the teacher to the head's room), or whether it is wiser to send another member of the class to request the head to come along to the room. Again, with a child who is this difficult, the head will already be aware of the problem and should therefore have agreed to this action on the teacher's part should it prove necessary. While the head is being fetched, instead of an icy pregnant silence while the teacher tries to outstare the child and hopes that the head will be prompt, the teacher carries straight on with the lesson from the point at which it was left off. Enough time has been wasted on the child, and now work must be resumed.

Confrontations of this magnitude are fortunately rare. But even where the teacher notes a mild degree of defiance in certain individual children this should be seen as an indication that action needs to be taken to prevent such defiance from recurring and perhaps worsening in the future. Essentially this means identifying the cause of the defiance (see Chapters 1 and 2). Are such children trying to draw attention themselves? Do they feel they have something to prove, either to themselves or to the rest of the class? Have they perhaps some reason, however misguided, for grievance against the teacher? Are they trying to defend feelings of inadequacy in the face of the tasks that the teacher is setting the class? Have they problems at home which they are tending to bring into the classroom? Whatever the reason, once it has been identified it becomes easier to know how to relate to the individuals concerned.

Opportunities must be taken to come to know them better.

Informal chats while they are helping the teacher to carry out tasks in the break or lunchtime, are again invaluable. At the same time as allowing the teacher to understand the child better, these allow the teacher to make his or her position clearer to the child. Classroom obedience is not something that the teacher demands as a way of demonstrating power over the children, simply something that is vital if a roomful of 30 or more people is to function successfully together and find interest and profit in the work available. If the child feels there is a grievance, then it must be discussed with the teacher afterwards. When trying to relate to 30 children at once, it may be that the teacher inadvertently passes over someone's problems, or appears to speak unnecessarily sharply to someone. No one is immune from mistakes. The teacher is always ready to discuss such matters with the individual or individuals concerned at the end of the lesson. If the child has a genuine reason for feeling slighted in front of the rest of the class, then the teacher will make it clear when the next lesson arrives that this was not intended. (Words to the effect that 'It may have looked last lesson as if I was having a go at Sonia over (such and such a matter). I wasn't, and I'm sorry if it looked that way'.) Some teachers find it very difficult to make what amounts to an apology to a child, fearing it indicates a loss of authority. In consequence they either avoid doing so in any circumstances, or do so very grudgingly, making it apparent to everyone how much the effort is costing them. Failure to apologize only confirms the children in their view that the teacher is unfair (and I stressed the importance of fairness earlier in the chapter), while a grudging apology can indeed lead to a loss of authority, since it indicates to the children that the teacher sees it as a humiliating climb down. An open and friendly recognition of error, on the other hand, along the lines of the example offered above, shows that the teacher does care about the feelings of children and places a high premium on fairness. Respect for the teacher and for the teacher's authority is likely to increase in consequence, while the children are also given an excellent example of how to behave in their own lives.

Physical aggression towards the teacher. In spite of certain well-publicized incidents, physical aggression towards the teacher is mercifully rare. But it does occur, though the stereotype of the undersized teacher being tackled by the hulking adolescent is less true perhaps than that of the nursery or first school teacher being scratched and pinched by a minute but determined spitfire. But whatever the size of the antagonist, it is rare indeed for physical aggression to be offered towards the teacher totally without warning and by a child who hitherto has been friendly and co-operative. Usually there have been clear warnings that the child has a fiery temper, or that for whatever reason he or she is building up a strong charge of resentment or frustration against the teacher, the rest of the class, or the school in general. Aware of what is happening, the teacher takes the kind of action outlined in the discussion on defiance to find out what is going wrong and to defuse the situation by sensible and positive action. More attempts are made to draw such children into things if they are feeling left out; the criticisms offered of their work are couched in more helpful and encouraging terms; more interest is shown in their progress and in any useful out of school activities in which they are involved; more opportunities are taken to commend their worthwhile efforts in class, and so on. With reasoned and appropriate actions of this kind, the teacher is usually able to ensure that things run little risk of developing into actual violence.

Violent incidents. However, if such violence does occur, the teacher has to have a strategy for response. It needs saying again that this response should not be one of anger. Easier to preach, certainly, than to put into practice. But unless the teacher is much bigger and stronger than the child, an angry response could have disastrous consequences, with the child becoming further inflamed in turn, and a wild flurry of fisticuffs developing to the visible and vocal delight of the rest of the class. Except in very unusual instances of extreme maladjustment (where the problem, as was suggested within the contexts of rudeness and defiance, should already have been identified by the school), a child who does strike a teacher usually feels immediately aghast at what has been done, however convincing the attempt to bluster it out afterwards. The first blow is therefore unlikely to be followed by another one unless the teacher becomes angry and hits back (perhaps more likely with a male than with a female teacher).

The best response is therefore calm and decisive action to take the heat out of the situation. Unless the child is unusually skilled or the teacher unusually lucky, the blow is unlikely to have actually felled the latter. The teacher therefore immediately steps back, not (hopefully) in fear but because if the child now wishes to strike again the decision has to be taken to close the space between him or her and the teacher; not an easy decision if the child is already feeling a degree of horror at the blow that has just been offered. Creating this physical space between teacher and child also indicates to the child that the teacher has no intention of mounting a threat of violence in return, and allows the teacher to be in a better position for self-defence should the child step forward and have another go.

Since this book is not a manual on the martial arts, I cannot go into details on how such an attempt at self-defence should be mounted, either if the child does decide to strike again or if the initial attack consists not of a single punch but of a general windmilling of arms in the direction of the teacher's face and body. But the simple action of raising the bent left arm, level with the chin, and allowing the child to rain blows on it while the bent right arm is held level with the midriff has the advantage of providing adequate protection while at the same time not appearing to offer aggression in return. At the same time (and this is essential) the child must be spoken to calmly and sensibly and told that you can see he or she is angry about something and if they will stop for a moment they can have a chance to explain. Thus the child is allowed to see that stopping the attack will lead to an immediate reward (the chance to have a say) rather than to any dire public retribution. Once the child has calmed a little, the teacher treats the whole matter in a matter-of-fact way, showing no sign of discomfort or worse still of being outraged by the incident, and that the intention now is to get things sorted out.

When the child has had a say, the teacher comments on what has been said and then adds words to the effect that 'But you can't just attack people, however strongly you happen to feel about something. In any case, this is going to take us a little time to sort out, so we'll talk about it at the end of the lesson.' When the end of the lesson comes, the teacher points out reasonably to the child that the headteacher will need to be involved, since he or she is bound to hear about the incident anyway, and it will be far better to hear about it from them, and to get the full story, than if the news comes in a garbled form from somebody else.

Of course it is open to the teacher to insist that the child accompanies him or her to the headteacher the moment the violence is over. But this risks a further outburst from the child. The whole issue is obviously delicately poised, and demands skillful judgement on the part of the teacher. It is better to be sure that tempers have sufficiently cooled before the child is told what has to be done. But in any case, when the chlid is taken to the headteacher it must not be a case of the classteacher now 'demanding' that the child be punished. The nature of the punishment must be left to the headteacher. Relationships between the teacher and the child are likely to be much better in the future if the latter is not left with the feeling that all the teacher really wanted was revenge, and had to rely upon the headteacher as the only one strong enough to deliver it.

Physical aggression between children. Rather more frequent than direct aggression towards the teacher are those occasions when the teacher has to step in and separate children fighting between themselves. This may happen in the playground, in the corridors or cloakrooms, or even in the classroom in the intervals between lessons (or, more rarely, during the lesson itself). Usually the teacher's firm instructions to the children to put a stop to their behaviour is all that is necessary. Often both children are secretly rather glad to have a good excuse to break off their fight, with honours left more or less even.

The secret again lies in calm and decisive action on the teacher's part. He or she homes swiftly in on the children and, using their names if these are known, calls a halt to proceedings. A simple statement ('Stop that immediately') is all that is required. Threats or vilifications are unnecessary, and only risk inflaming the children further. They are already well enough aware that what they are doing is against the school rules, and the teacher's firmness of manner is far more important in putting a stop to things than are promises of punishment. Once the children have calmed down a little, the teacher asks for an explanation, either there and then or at the end of the lesson as appropriate. It is important to listen carefully to this explanation, allowing each child to feel he or she has had a fair hearing. The brusque refusal by some teachers in this situation to listen to what the children have to say leaves the children as frustrated and angry as ever and this time with a grudge against the teacher as well. The teacher's object should not be one of retribution so much as one of conciliation. Children have to learn how to handle their angry feelings without resorting to violence, and one simple lesson on how to articulate and reconcile their differences to two children who have just been at each other's throats, is of far more value than any amount of abstract theorizing to a class on the evils of aggression.

In the unusual event of the children refusing to break off their battle when told to do so by the teacher, the teacher is now faced with having to intervene physically. This is not so daunting as it sounds, provided the teacher does not do so either timidly on the one hand or with hostility on the other. Timidity invites the children either to ignore the teacher or push him or her to one side, while hostility can invite one or both of the children to turn their violence against the teacher. Instead the teacher decides swiftly on which of the children appears to be the aggressor or to be getting the upper hand, and pulls them firmly but not roughly clear. If necessary, the child can then be restrained by arms wrapped around the body, thus pinning the arms, and by holding on tightly. To do this effectively, the teacher needs to stand to the side of the child, thus avoiding the dangers of a reflex kick to the shins, and to hold the child close, minimizing the chances of an elbow in the ribs and allowing the child no freedom to manoeuvre. At the same time (and this is essential) the teacher talks calmly and firmly to the child, commenting that it is clear they are very angry about something, and must cool down and explain what it is. Should the other child attempt to use this opportunity to aim a blow at the now immobilized opponent, the teacher speaks to him or her much more sharply, telling them to cut it out and they will be given every chance to have a say as well in due course.

Unless there is a school rule to the effect that all fighting must be reported to the headteacher, there is no need to feel that the two children who have been fighting must automatically receive some form of punishment once things have been sorted out. Obviously the teacher wishes to deter any further outbreaks of violence, but punishment is unlikely to be the best way of doing this. As I have already said, the aim of the teacher is to help children handle their angry feelings without fighting about things. And helping them to air these feelings in an understanding and constructive way is of more use than handing out some meaningless sanction such as an imposition or detention. The use of sanctions of this kind, which are imposed after the event and after things have been talked through, is bound to look to the children suspiciously like punishment for punishment's sake. The effect might be not to attack their readiness to fight again next time the occasion arises but their respect for the teacher and for his or her ability to understand their problems.

Hyperactivity. Hyperactivity is a word that is difficult to define precisely, but it refers to those children who have a very small concentration span and who seem incapable of sitting still or of settling to a given task for anything but the briefest of intervals. They are constantly to be found turning around, roaming around the classroom, interrupting the work of others, unable to leave anything that comes within reach alone, and quite incapable of listening to what the teacher has to say for more than two words together. Extreme hyperactivity is classified in fact as a form of maladjustment, and is often to be found along with a constellation of other maladjusted traits. But in a slightly less obtrusive form it is encountered all too often in children, particularly young children, and differs from normal over-activity in that the child appears to have no self-control, however hard the effort is made.

Hyperactivity at one time used to be seen as a symptom of brain damage, but these days there is held usually to be no known single cause (though allergies to certain items of diet are now being suggested in some quarters as of possible importance). What is not in doubt however is the effect that hyperactivity can have upon teachers, busy as they are with 30 other children as well. The hyperactive child literally wears the teacher out. The latter develops the feeling that the whole day is spent in a fruitless attempt to get the child concerned to sit quietly for even the briefest of intervals, or to desist from interfering with what the others are doing or to obey the simplest instructions to leave certain forbidden items alone. In a nursery or infant school, where there is a great deal of movement within the class anyway, such a child can cause the severest of problems and the severest of strains upon the teacher.

Unfortunately there is no simple answer to hyperactivity. Since the child genuinely appears unable to control what he or she is doing, punishment is both inappropriate and unproductive, though when in *extremis* the teacher may often resort to it. Putting the child to sit on his or her own has little effect, since hyperactive children cannot stay seated for any length of time. Physically restraining hyperactive children is no better, since it often leads to struggles and tantrums. Sending the child to the headteacher is only effective in that it gets the child out of the room (a not insignificant mercy), but only to be returned sooner or later. Indeed sooner rather than later, as the headteacher's nerves in turn become stretched to breaking point and the headteacher's study rendered less and less habitable.

The major factor to bear in mind when dealing with hyperactive children is that some clear specialist assessment of their problems must be obtained at the earliest opportunity. The definition of hyperactivity is not a precise one, but the educational psychologist, having interviewed the child and carried out appropriate testing procedures, will be in a position to advise the teacher on whether the child is simply a particularly lively specimen or whether there is a more fundamental problem. Once a child has been placed in the hyperactive category, then the teacher must accept that he or she is someone (more often a boy than a girl, though either sex can be involved) who is unlikely to respond to many routine control strategies. The child's short attention span, extreme distractability, impaired rate of learning, compulsive fidgeting and physical movement make it very difficult for the teacher to exercise the necessary guidance over his or her behaviour, and therefor the teacher must revise expectations accordingly.

In the view of some psychologists (though it is not easy to see how to go about obtaining firm evidence for or against) the observed link between hyperactivity and maladjustment is often caused by the extreme frustration that hyperactive children experience when their need for physical movement is constantly thwarted by those in authority. Thus the wise teacher is the one who does not make a difficult situation intolerable by constantly demanding behaviour from such children which they are quite incapable of producing. Instead, things are carefully planned so that the children are given as much scope as possible for their need for physical activity short of seriously disrupting the rest of the class. Few hyperactive children can sustain their own company for any length of time, so putting individuals in a corner of the classroom, even with plenty to keep them occupied, is rarely the answer. Far better to organize activities around them, putting them to work or play with different groups of children for short intervals of time, and encouraging the other children to participate in the attempt to keep them occupied. Because hyperactive children tend (for obvious reasons) not to make close friends this is demanding a lot of the rest of the class, but since the presence of a hyperactive child is likely to disrupt work anyway, it is far better for everyone if they are drawn into ongoing activities and kept involved than if they are excluded and left to force a way into things on their own terms.

The maladjusted child. Discussion of maladjustment *per se* lies outside the scope of this book. Special techniques are required for the assessment and treatment of maladjustment, and the problems posed by such children go beyond those of normal class control. Nevertheless, the line between maladjustment and consistently bad behaviour is a somewhat arbitrary one, and even the term 'maladjustment', because of its vague nature and pejorative overtones, is now passing into disuse. Global terms such as 'maladjustment' are in any event of very limited help since they give us no clue as to the real nature of the child's problem. Is he or she an extreme isolate for example? Or violent and aggressive? Or subject to emotional outbursts? Or given to acts of vandalism? Or to theft or arson or to any other activity which in an adult would be classified as criminal?

The teacher's main concern in the face of the child who presents extreme problems of the kind exemplified above is to obtain outside help. Such help will not only be of benefit to the teacher, but will more importantly assist the child in coming to terms with his or her own problems. As soon as the teacher has identified a child who poses special difficulties, the attention of the headteacher should be sought. Some teachers have the feeling that to admit to having a child in the class with whom they cannot fully cope is to admit to professional weakness. Nothing could be further from the truth. It is in fact the weak teacher, caught up in a sense of personal failure and unable to be fully objective about what is going on, who will attempt to hide problems from colleagues, and will not recognize the disservice that is in consequence being done both to the problem child and to the rest of the class.

I have already fully discussed the way in which teachers can use each other as resources (Chapter 6), but there are also resources outside the school that are readily available. Through the headteacher, the first step is usually to contact the school psychological service, who will assess the child using appropriate standardized measures and interview techniques. The school psychologist will then co-operate with the school in devising strategies (based upon those discussed in Chapters 4 and 5) for relating to the child, and will help to monitor future progress. In many cases, it will also be appropriate to involve the social services if the child comes from a difficult background. The social worker will visit the home, and relay information to the school on the influences and conditions operating upon the child from parents and other caretakers. The school welfare officer, or whoever is responsible for school attendance will normally be involved as a matter of course if there has been evidence of persistent truanting, and will also be a helpful resource, since he or she too will have evidence of the home and of the child's background. If the child has been before the courts, there may also be a juvenile liaison officer involved, while the community police officer (if there is one) may be another person with useful information to contribute. If the child's behaviour is particularly disturbed, he or she may be referred for psychiatric treatment, either through the school psychological service or through the general practitioner, and the psychiatrist may therefore be yet another person with a valuable part to play. Particularly in communities where there is a strong element of religious observance, the parish priest or equivalent could be a further important source of information and influence upon the child's home, and his moral authority is of particular help when dealing with certain sets of parents.

Once a child has been referred to the headteacher as representing a particular control problem, it is now the headteacher's task to contact the child's parents and, if necessary, the various other agencies mentioned above. Case conferences can then take place, and decisions reached as to how best to help the child. It could be that the whole family will be urged to attend a family therapy unit, if one is available. Or it may be that the child will attend regular counselling sessions at the school psychological service or with the psychiatrist. But whatever the outcome, it is important that the child is made aware that the school is functioning as a helping agency, rather than as yet another set of problems with which to cope. The very experience of realizing that the school is there to help rather than to make things worse is likely, in itself, to lessen some of the antagonism that the child has hitherto been manifesting. The provision of performance contracts (Chapter 4), or counselling sessions within the school either mounted by the headteacher or by a member of staff with particular responsibility for pastoral care, are direct ways in which the school can demonstrate its concern for the child and its practical value in guiding him or her towards a more responsible and rewarding life.

A class out of control. Strategies such as those discussed in this book will ensure that the teacher is unlikely to find a class erupting into the kind of concerted action which it is difficult to contain. However, there may well be occasions when near riotous behaviour of this kind is found to be going on in a neighbouring classroom which for some reason has been left untended. The teacher arrives to find missiles being exchanged across the room, children shouting and singing, and various intense little scuffles going on in all quarters. Usually the redeeming feature here is that, in spite of the noise, the whole thing is good-humoured and friendly. The children have seen an opportunity to enjoy themselves, and are taking it. It is only where physical aggression is taking place, an eventuality with which I have already dealt in this chapter, that the teacher may have to intervene physically in order to bring things back to normal.

Faced, therefore, with a situation that looks like bedlam but is essentially good-humoured, the teacher is unlikely to experience real problems. The teacher's simple presence in the doorway may do the trick, particularly if the children near at hand, who are the first to spot him or her and calm down, are influential members of the class. But a preferable strategy is for the teacher to make this presence known to everyone immediately. This involves walking decisively into the room and doing something to draw attention such as calling out or clapping your hands or banging the board rubber on the desk. As was stressed in Chapter 5, it is always of more value if the individual names of a child or of children can be called out, rather than resorting to a general command. If the child or children concerned are known to be prestigious members of the class, so much the better. And the effect is better still if instead of simply calling to the child or children to stop the noise, they are told to do something positive. 'Benson and Turner, come here at once' is better than 'Benson and Turner, stop that noise', though the teacher must be careful not to call upon the only two members of the class who are unlikely to respond immediately to whatever is demanded of them. At all times, but particularly when facing a whole class in a state of uproar, the issuing of a forceful order which is then ignored by the children concerned immediately weakens one's authority. So the golden rule is to issue an order which one is confident will be heeded. In extreme cases, call out the names of the more sensible members of the class. As these children fall silent, joined by most of the others, the real troublemakers will become readily apparent, and the teacher can now walk firmly across to them and demand they put a stop to their misbehaviour as well.

If the teacher knows no one in the class, and is in addition unsure of the ability to restore order, then it is more sensible to go quickly to summon the deputy head (or someone else responsible for discipline) than to take on the class single-handed and meet defeat. News travels all too quickly in a school, particularly if it is bad news from the teacher's point of view, and the information that Mr or Mrs Smith made an ineffectual and humiliating attempt to quell a riot in 4R will be relayed with glee from ear to ear before the day is out, thus seriously weakening the standing of the hapless Mr or Mrs Smith for some months to come. But if the teacher is confident, then there is no reason why even not knowing the names of the members of 4R should prove an insuperable obstacle. The technique once again is to enter the room decisively and immediately make one's presence felt, either by a clap of the hands or a bang on the desk of the ubiquitous board rubber. A loud roar of 'Quiet!' seems impressive in theory, but if the children stubbornly refuse to be quiet, then we come back to the point of the previous paragraph: an order which is ignored by the children immediately weakens one's authority.

The clap of the hands does not represent the same total commitment of authority as does the bellow for quiet (it is also kinder on the vocal chords). Instead, it is a way of announcing one's arrival, a clearing of the decks for further action should such action be necessary.

Often this action is not necessary, but where it is the teacher adopts a second attention seeking strategy. Many of the children will now be aware of the teacher and will have stopped what they were doing, so the teacher quickly identifies the epicentre of the remaining disturbance, walks quickly over to it and taking the arm of the child concerned abstracts him or her out to the front of the class. The sheer surprise value of the teacher's action, plus the fact that this action is not offered in a particularly threatening or hostile way, is usually sufficient to ensure compliance. The child's arm is held firmly but not roughly and some semi-humorous remark like 'When in doubt always go for the strongest first' not only keeps things on a fairly light-hearted level but avoids any suggestion that the child concerned is being humiliated in front of friends.

Now that the class is silent, the teacher makes no particular issue out of what has just been happening. The children are told to sit down, and the child who was at the centre of things is simply told 'that includes you too'. No attempt is made to find out the cause of the disturbance, unless damage of some kind has been done. The disturbance was simply the consequence of a group of high-spirited youngsters being left untended for too long. And most of us, if we are honest, would have been in the thick of it were we still their age. Questions like 'Who started all that?' are unlikely to meet with an answer, and in a sense only invite secret derision from the class, since they indicate to the children how completely the teacher has misunderstood what was happening and what a gulf there is in consequence between them. I stressed in Chapter 5 the importance of remembering what it was like to be a child. In this case, if the teacher tries to remember, he or she will recall that these disturbances seem to arise spontaneously. The actual incidents that sparked them off, even if anyone can recall what they were, are immaterial. If it had not been those incidents then it would have been other similar ones. Thus by playing the role of outraged accuser, and demanding 'an answer' to questions about who was to blame, the teacher is only appearing slightly foolish. Since the chances are that the answer will not be forthcoming, there is also once again a risk of a loss of authority. Even if someone, wearied of the teacher's behaviour, eventually owns up, the 'confession' will be virtually meaningless, since the whole class was in fact involved. And if the teacher now hands out a punishment to the child, this will only serve to make the latter something of a hero in the eyes of the others, and to confirm everyone in their view that teachers are a peculiarly short-sighted and unfair species of life.

Far better, then, having won a decisive victory in quelling the riot for the teacher now to win everyone's further respect by treating the incident as over and done with. The children will be told to behave more sensibly in future, and the colleague who should have been responsible for the class and whose absence has been the predetermining factor in the children's behaviour will be sent for. If possible, the teacher will remain with the children until he or she comes, thus ensuring that there is no repetition of what has just been happening. Each time an incident of this kind occurs and is dealt with firmly and sensibly, the teacher's stock with the children concerned and with the school in general will rise, making it progressively easier to deal with similar occurrences in the future.

References

For teacher qualities and other important issues see: Burns, R. (1982) *Self Concept Development and Education.* London: Holt, Rinehart and Winston.

For maladjustment in the classroom see: Galloway, D.M. and Goodwin, C. (1976) (2nd edn) *Educating Slow Learning and Maladjusted Children.* London: Longman.

Chapter 8

Teacher Self-Perceptions and Self-Management

My purpose in this final chapter is to help teachers think a little more clearly about their own reactions to problems of class control and the way in which these reactions relate to the view individuals have of themselves as people and as teachers. For example, if we encounter a problem of class control, do we see it as a direct reflection of our own inabilities, both personal or professional, or do we see it as one of the unavoidable challenges of being a teacher? If the former, then we are likely to end up dispirited and discouraged, with consequent loss of self-esteem. If the latter, we are likely to remain positive and confident, with a clear belief in our own abilities to find a solution to whatever it is that is going wrong. To take a further example. Do we see an act of rudeness or defiance in a child as a direct threat to our prestige and authority, or do we see it as an indication that the child has a confused and counterproductive notion of how best to relate to people? If the former, then we are likely to react with defensiveness and anger, perhaps making a bad situation worse. If the latter, we are able to remain objective and take clear decisions as to what action is necessary.

These examples indicate once again the importance of a theme which has run right through this book, namely that when considering how problems of class control arise, and either intensify or are successfully dealt with, we must take into account not just the behaviour of the children but that of the teacher as well. In the examples in the above paragraph it can be seen clearly enough that when faced by similar situations, different teachers will react in different ways, and that this reaction will be determined not just by how the teacher reads the situation but by how the teacher views him or herself. Generally, the more confident and self-possessed the teacher, the more self-accepting and realistic, the more objective and clear about personal abilities and limitations, the more effective the teacher will be in responding to problems of class control. Even in particularly difficult circumstances, effective teachers of this kind have a better chance of remaining calm and resourceful, and are far less likely to punish themselves afterwards with feelings of helpless frustrated rage or of guilt and humiliating failure. They are able to accept that inevitably there are limitations upon what can be achieved with certain groups of children, and upon their own pro-fessional competence and skills. Set-backs will therefore neither be seen as frustrating nor as daunting, but simply as opportunities to learn more about children, about oneself, and about the art of teaching. Similarly, they are able to recognize that misbehaviour by a child should not be seen as a personal affront to one's own dignity, nor as yet another indication of one's own inadequacy. Neither response is of the least positive help. And should either response occur, then they are able to analyse it carefully, as indicated in due course below, and find a way of avoiding such personally and professionally damaging reactions in the future. I now look in turn at the two major issues that are involved in any discussion of such reactions and of other negative reactions linked closely to them.

'Fear' of class control problems

When facing a new class for the first time, or when facing one with which we have had difficulties in the past, we most of us naturally feel some measure of fear (or anxiety if you prefer, but fear is often the more appropriate word). This fear makes us nervous and uncertain, prompting us frequently to make mistakes that normally we would avoid. We may confuse children's names for example, lose our place in lesson notes, snap unnecessarily at the class or at individuals, make errors on the blackboard, hand out wild threats, dry up in the middle of a sentence, forget important points that we intended to bring out, blush and bluster, and generally make a pretty woeful exhibition of ourselves. All these shortcomings will be noted with interest by the class, who will then set to work collectively and as individuals to exploit them to maximum effect. Whatever else children are unable to do, there is no doubting their talents in this direction. They appear able with unerring accuracy to target in on all those areas where the teacher is most vulnerable, and often to show a hearty disregard for the gentle virtues of understanding and compassion.

Clearly what has happened is that the teacher's very fear of the class has caused precisely the blunders that produce the child behaviours of which he or she was originally afraid. So what can be done about this fear? Whole books have been written about lesser subjects, and it would be unrealistic to pretend that there is any simple answer. However, there is a range of strategies which, if remembered and consistently applied, will help to reduce and even finally eliminate the problem:

Fear is a natural reaction when facing a threatening situation for many people. It is nothing to be ashamed of, and the more we feel such shame the less chance we often have to deal with the fear objectively and sensibly. A more constructive reaction is to see the fear not as a sign of weakness but as a perfectly normal response which we can handle by perfectly normal means. By accepting our fear in this way, and recognizing that it is something with which we can deal, we remove the *fear of fear*.

It helps to analyse fear. We are perhaps used to thinking 'I feel afraid', but of what does the 'being afraid' actually consist? Certain physical symptoms such as butterflies in the stomach perhaps and dryness in the throat. Analyse the fear and identify the symptoms that indicate fear, just as in Chapter 4 I analysed the actual elements that go to make up a child's bad behaviour.

Having analysed these symptoms, practise not identifying with them. Usually as soon as we feel the butterflies or the pounding heart rate that indicates fear, we identify with these things and register the information 'I am afraid'. Thus we now, as the grammar of the statement 'I am afraid' indicates, allow ourselves in a very real sense to *become* our fear. The fear and the person who is experiencing the fear become at the practical level one and the same thing. Practise, instead, simply observing these symptoms of fear with the detachment that one would observe any other everyday phenomena in the outside world.

Of great assistance in this process of non-identification with fear symptoms is the ability to identify instead with some non-stressful bodily activity. The most effective one to choose is your breathing. When nervous we often find ourselves taking short, gasping breaths, but this is something over which we have direct control. Consciously restore the breathing to its usual steady rhythm; breathe just a little deeper than usual, since the body has a particular need for oxygen when stressed, but do not take the deep, shuddering breaths that people sometimes attempt when trying to 'calm' their nerves.

The breathing should be as near normal as possible, and one then concentrates simply upon the breath entering and leaving the nostrils or upon the gentle rise and fall of one's chest or abdomen. This can be practised when sitting quietly in the staffroom before going to a particular lesson, then continued as one walks to the lesson and enters the classroom. Note that the concentration should be upon the breathing itself, rather than upon the nervous feelings in the chest wall and abdomen. The air itself as it enters the body is not in the least bit anxious. It is cool and calm as ever, and it is upon this coolness and calmness that the concentration is allowed to rest.

At all times, practise breathing from the abdomen rather than from the chest. Breathing is initiated by the diaphragm, a sheet of powerful muscle that separates the chest cavity from the lower abdomen. The natural way to breathe is therefore from low down rather than from high up. Watch a baby breathing, and note where his or her body rises and falls with each breath. As we grow older, and particularly if we are nervous or tense, we tend to breath increasingly from high up in the chest, a practice which does nothing to help us relax. Practise breathing from as low down as possible, relaxing all the accumulated tension in the abdominal muscles at the same time. By drawing the breath down rather than hunching it up into the upper chest, we also allow the shoulders and neck, common centres of tension, to relax.

Having arrived at the lesson in a less anxious state than usual, try to maintain this desirable state of affairs. This is done by monitoring one's own behaviour and endeavouring to analyse the symptoms of one's anxiety in the way outlined above. Usually when we are in a nervous state with a class we become so caught up in meeting the challenges presented by the children that we lose sight of what is happening to our own bodies until it is suddenly borne in on us how badly our head is aching and how tightly stretched is our every nerve. But though our awareness of these things may be sudden, in fact they have been building up gradually. By monitoring ourselves carefully, and with a little practice, we can become conscious of these symptoms at an early stage, when it is still possible to relax them again. At the first sign of tensions in the shoulders we can gently let them go. At the first sign of tightness in the stomach muscles we can release it. At the first sign of shallow, hurried breathing, we can deepen and relax it and so on. By consciously letting go of tensions at the point at which they arise, we can relieve the body of so much of the stress that exhausts us and sends further alarm signals to the brain.

Practise deliberately slowing things down. When we become anxious in front of a class of children, we often tend increasingly to rush things. Any pause in the proceedings worries us, so we fill it with meaningless sounds like 'er' or 'um' (which, as suggested in Chapter 3, the children will soon take to counting if we overdo it), or we talk even more quickly than usual, straining our voice in an effort to be heard and matching the tense, staccato nature of our speech by the staccato nature of our movements and gestures. The remedy is to make a conscious effort at all times to slow down. Without becoming over-deliberate, the teacher must have sufficient confidence (see Chapter 5) to take things at their proper pace. Often a pause in what we are saying, provided it is not too long, is a useful way of refocusing attention upon the teacher. It also allows the teacher that brief interval for marshalling thoughts, for taking a proper breath, for relaxing the muscles and the throat, for looking around the room and registering what children are doing, for meeting and holding the gaze of individuals and giving them an encouraging smile, and for demonstrating to him or herself that things are under control and that mayhem is not likely to break out every time there is a momentary lull in the proceedings.

Analyse what it is that prompts the feelings of fear. Of what are we actually afraid? Physical violence? Rudeness? Outright defiance? A class riot? As I have indicated in the book already, careful planning and organization, together with clear strategies for dealing with these eventualities should they arise, go much of the way towards removing the need for such fear. The well-prepared teacher is far less likely to encounter such threats than the ill-prepared teacher, or to be nonplussed in the face of them But if we analyse the fear a little deeper, we may find that what actually prompts the anxiety is not so much the direct confrontation posed by the child as the teacher's fear of personal humiliation at being unable to deal with it. That is, the teacher's fear that there will be loss of self-esteem and loss of esteem in the eyes of the children. Again, when such a fear is looked at closely the need for it is seen to be unnecessary. From the self-esteem perspective, no teacher should automatically think the worse of him or herself every time things go badly in the classroom.

However naturally gifted a teacher may be, there are always occasions when control problems arise and are not conclusively dealt with, particularly when the teacher is inexperienced. Teaching can at times be a difficult and demanding job, just as it can at other (more frequent) times be a rewarding and stimulating one. Often the teacher has to contend with adverse circumstances, such as a large class or a lack of equipment (see Chapters 3 and 6), or with children who have received little guidance and support from their families (see Chapter 2). Things cannot be expected always to go well under such circumstances, and there is little to be gained by the teacher always blaming him or herself for not being able to cope expertly. The important thing is to analyse afterwards what went wrong and why, and see what lessons can be learnt from it for the future. When did things start becoming out of hand? What sparked them off? An action by the teacher or by the class? And how did the teacher react? Why did that prove ineffective? What happened next? And so on. Such an analysis should be carried out objectively, unemotionally, and with a readiness to see the humour in the situation, even if the laugh does seem to be rather upon the teacher. The information that it reveals then helps the teacher to decide what to do when similar situations occur next time.

From the point of view of loss of esteem in the eyes of the children, it is vital to remember that children are realistic enough to know, even in the primary school, that teaching is not an easy job, and that no teacher can always be expected to have the right answer to problems of class control. A teacher does not forfeit respect simply because he or she has trouble in the classroom from time to time. The loss of respect comes from blustering, the ill-considered threats, the impotent rage, the futile commands and the clearly shattered composure of the badly-prepared teacher. Teachers who remain calm and objective, and obviously in full control of themselves even if not of the class, have much less to fear in this regard. The class will appreciate not only that their behaviour has failed to hurt the teacher, but that the latter has a coolness and a resilience that they can admire and envy. The more the teacher is thus seen as a desirable role model for the class, the less he or she is likely to be seen as a deserving target for their bad behaviour.

The need for patience with oneself. The teacher must not, of course, always expect rapid results. Dealing with our fears and anxieties is rarely a speedy process, since we are dealing with something very fundamental to our way of responding to the world. But the teacher must be alert to each small advance, and never give way to discouragement. The practice of concentrating upon the breathing, for example, may have little observable results the first few times. We may quickly find our attention switching back to our nervous symptoms. But it is important not, therefore, to write it off as a failure. If we take up a new sport or a new handicraft we expect to have to practise it confidently and assiduously many times before we begin to master the skills involved. Yet too often we expect to make radical changes in our psychological life simply by applying a new technique for the first time. This is unrealistic. But if we carry on with the technique sensibly and conscientiously, it will not be that long before we start seeing the first signs of very welcome results.

'Anger' at class control problems

The second major issue involved in a teacher's reactions to class control problems is that of anger. Fear and anger (flight and fight responses respectively) are the two natural ways in which we react to threats, but both are likely to prove counter-productive when those threats appear to come from a class of children. We cannot just run away from these threats, however much we may feel like it at the time, and fear must therefore be dealt with, as I discussed in the last section. But we cannot fight either, so the anger that gears us up for this fighting must inevitably be repressed and frustrated, leaving us raging inwardly and prone to the kind of errors in relation to anger discussed in Chapters 5 and 6. Far better to get to know more about our own anger, as I suggested should be done with fear, and learn how to handle it and eventually prevent it even from arising.

A good place at which to start is the first of the points listed under fear. That is:

See the anger as a natural reaction, but one which is little help in the context of class control, and one which can be dealt with by perfectly normal means.

As with fear, analyse the anger. When we become angry, of what does the anger consist? A hot feeling in the belly or in the head? A surge of violent energy? A desire to hit out at someone? Once analysed, again, as with fear, the next step is to cease identifying with these feelings. Usually with anger we either let it take us over or we try to force it back down from whence it came. Ceasing to identify with the angry feeling means simply letting it arise and pass away without letting it touch that calm part of the mind that is doing the observing. Easier said than done of course, and harder for many people to do with anger than with fear, but again practice is a great help, particularly when allied with the following two strategies.

When in a relaxed frame of mind, practise visualizing and reliving the situations that usually arouse anger. Observe them calmly, maintaining the relaxed frame of mind (this strategy is also helpful when dealing with fear). Should anger start to stir, discontinue the visualization, turn to something more soothing, and return to the visualization only when the anger has passed. If this exercise proves a little difficult at first, start with visualizing a scene that only causes minor annoyance. When this can be contemplated in the relaxed state, then progress to a slightly more arousing scene and so on. The exercise should never be hurried. One scene coped with each time the exercise is attempted is quite enough. But with practice, the relaxed frame of mind in which one confronts the imaginary situation will carry over into the real situation. The anger will cease to arise, and the individual will gradually come to realize that he or she has far more power over the emotional state than was once thought.

Again as with fear, analyse why one tends to become angry in given situations. What is it about them that leads to arousal? Is it the feeling that the child is threatening one's authority? Is it one's ego and false sense of importance that is under attack? Is it that one attributes motives of nastiness to the child which he or she may not really be feeling? Is it that one feels made to look foolish in front of the class? Is one wary of the reactions of colleagues if they get to hear that one allowed a child to behave in the manner concerned? Is the anger simply another way of expressing fear? And so on. Once the reasons for the anger are analysed, it may become clear that it is primarily a defence against one's own bruised feelings of dignity. Certainly children cannot be allowed to speak rudely to teachers, but we cannot deal with this rudeness if we take it as a personal insult. View the rudeness or defiance or whatever it may be impersonally, simply as a strategy that the child is trying on against a member of staff, and a strategy which he or she must now be allowed to see is not effective in gaining the desired end, whatever that end may be (and often this end is simply to make the teacher angry). Again rehearsing and visualizing scenes in which rudeness is involved, and practising an impersonal and calm response, is an invaluable help.

Teacher stress in relation to class control

Teaching, because of the constant legitimate demands of the

children and the volume of work involved, can be a stressful job, even at the best of times. But problems of class control can add very greatly to the stresses involved; in fact such problems are probably the most potent source of stress in the teacher's professional life, no matter what the age-groups being taught. By temperament, some people seem to feel this stress more keenly than others, but no matter who is involved, there are (as with fear and anger) various things that the teacher can do to lessen the pressures involved. Indeed unless these pressures are reduced, the teacher is likely to become increasingly tired and tense as the term wears on. The major thing of course is to improve the ability to maintain good class control, and such improvement is the aim of this book. Improved class control leads to increased confidence on the part of the teacher, increased learning on the part of the children, and increased enjoyment in the lesson for both teacher and class. But while the teacher is developing skills at class control, there are other helpful factors upon which he or she can work. These can be summarized as follows.

Reduce the emotional strain caused respectively by fear and anger, using the kind of strategies already described in this chapter.

Do not dwell on failures and mistakes. See these simply as useful learning opportunities. Analyse what went wrong and why, determine ways of avoiding such eventualities in the future, then put the whole subject out of your mind. The tendency to brood over mistakes, to relive with a hot flush of embarrassment that awful moment with 4R only prolongs the feeling of strain, and makes it harder to meet 4R again next lesson with equanimity.

Cultivate a sense of humour. Learn to chuckle over errors when they happen and when they are reviewed in the way suggested in the last paragraph. It is sometimes claimed that humour is the ability to recognize the gap between pretension and performance. As teachers, we often have high pretensions, entering the classroom with a flourish and expecting things to go well. When we make less than an effective job of them, there is certainly humour in the situation, therefore, even if the laugh is upon ourselves. The ability to laugh at oneself, in private even if not in public, is a good way of releasing emotional tension. The teacher who takes him or herself too seriously is missing a useful strategy for unwinding at the end of the day.

Keep expectations realistic, both in terms of the children and in terms of oneself. This is a point that I have stressed a number of times, and it is almost as important within the context of reducing personal tensions as it is in avoiding tensions within the class. If we constantly expect too much of children in class control terms, keeping a mental image of a class working diligently and silently, with every child and every thing in its place, and pupils responding obediently and politely with a tug of a metaphorical forelock every time they are spoken to, then we are in for constant strain as we try to translate this image into reality, and constant frustration as we find the task impossible. It is in the nature of children to be noisy and untidy at times, to speak discourteously at times, and try to get away on occasions with not doing as they are told. It is also, incidentally, as well to remember that it is sometimes the very qualities we find hardest to relate to in children that make them most effective as adults. We often admire a determined, outspoken and courageous adult, for example, yet find these qualities very uncomfortable in children. However, by recognizing what it is possible and not possible to expect from children, the teacher can avoid strains and frustrations of this kind. Similarly by accepting that even teachers can only do their best, and cannot be expected always to do things perfectly, we avoid blaming ourselves for things that are less our fault than due simply to inexperience or perhaps to the kind of conditions under which the teacher sometimes has to work.

Learn and practise physical relaxation techniques. I have already discussed these in this chapter. The teacher must practise such techniques at home, between lessons, and even during the lessons themselves. By becoming aware of breathing, and of the build-up and release of tensions in the muscles, the teacher becomes not only mentally better equipped to cope with a class but also much less tired physically. Anxiety and nervous tension burn up a great deal of physical energy between them. And one area that must receive particular attention is the voice. The tense person tends to use the voice wrongly, particularly if it has to be raised over the noise of the class. Instead of allowing the voice, as with the breathing, to be initiated by the movement of the diaphragm, the voice comes from a frantic straining of the muscles of the throat itself. Not surprisingly the voice becomes hoarse (perhaps permanently, with nodules on the vocal chords), the throat sore, and the whole body tensed up in sympathy. Proper use of the voice can best be taught by a manual on speech therapy, or better still by a speech therapist, but I raise the point here because all too often the teacher is sadly unaware that things are going wrong.

Share one's problems with colleagues. I talked in Chapter 6 about the value of teachers using each other as a resource. But far too often the teacher feels that difficulties in the classroom must be hidden away from the rest of the staff. Perhaps there is the feeling that one will be judged professionally wanting if colleagues come to hear of these difficulties. However, the teacher who claims never to have problems of control is either very lucky or very self-deluded. Unless they teach in a sheltered environment, all teachers meet a particular class or a particular child from time to time who they feel poses a special threat. The more sympathetic and helpful colleagues are with each other's difficulties, the more supportive and encouraging, then the better able is the individual teacher to face and overcome professional worries. Teaching can be a somewhat isolated profession, with each teacher only seeing fellow members of staff for a short time each day, so it is important that individual teachers and the staff as a whole create the right opportunities for consultation and for mutual professional assistance.

Similarly, opportunities should be taken to discuss problems with family and friends. There is little point in bottling up professional anxieties when there are sympathetic folk around us who would be happy to offer support and encouragement. Obviously other people will soon weary of us if we are constantly bemoaning our professional lot, but constructive discussions with them can be a great help towards seeing ourselves objectively and working out effective strategies for the future. Most people, particularly if they are close to us emotionally, are ready to listen to us if they can see we are making appropriate efforts to help ourselves, and if we are equally willing to listen to them in our own turn when they have problems.

Conclusion

The points raised in this chapter, and indeed throughout the book, are designed to help the teacher function more effectively in relationship with the class and with the self. If class control becomes a major obstacle for the teacher, with each lesson a kind of battleground and the teacher left tense and exhausted by the time the bell goes, then little in the way of real learning is likely to take place. Learning, and the creative response to learning, flourish best in an environment where children and teacher are united in their interest and enthusiasm for what is being taught, and share a bond of mutual respect and understanding. Such an environment rarely arises spontaneously. It depends in large measure upon the professional and personal skills of the teacher. Such skills, as I have tried to indicate in this book, can be acquired by teachers if they go about the business sensibly and methodically, with a willingness to analyse carefully what is going on both within the class and within themselves. There is rarely a short-cut to the development of any worthwhile teaching skill, and the skill of good class control is no exception. Much depends upon hard work, upon a belief in oneself, upon a willingness to learn from whatever experience happens to come along whether it be successful or unsuccessful, and upon a refusal to become discouraged. Many of the most effective teachers now at work in both primary and secondary schools had serious difficulties at the outset of their careers. In the days when people used to go in for such research, it was established by a number of studies that the degree of success shown by a student on final teaching practice showed little correlation with their success in the profession five years later. Many of those who have to struggle hardest initially end up amongst the best teachers in the long run.

The message therefore is clear. See class control problems, when they arise, simply as one of the integral aspects of the teacher's job, an aspect that can and will be mastered if the willingness and determination on the part of the teacher are there. With such mastery, the enjoyment and rewards that come from teaching increase by leaps and bounds. The teacher is a craftsman, engaged in one of the most honourable of all crafts, guiding and stimulating the development of children. Naturally enough, such an important craft requires study and dedication if one is to be successful at it, but equally such a craft repays the craftsman for his or her skills with a depth of satisfaction that few other professions can offer. Good class control is one of the most vital of these skills, a skill indeed upon which many of the other skills intimately depend. Ultimately, the good teacher is invariably a person who has acquired this skill. Initially, the good teacher is invariably a person who works towards acquiring it. And the more objective, focused and informed this work happens to be, then the more sure and more rapid the process of acquisition.

References

For self-understanding see: Klinke, C.L. (1978) *Self-Perception: The Psychology of Personal Awareness.* San Francisco: W.H. Freeman.

Kegan, R. (1982) *The Evolving Self: Problem and Process in Human Development.* Cambridge, Mass.: Harvard University Press.

Food for Thought:
Some Topics for Reflection and Debate

One of the most important aspects of the skillful teacher is the ability to think carefully about what is happening in the classroom and to learn from the things that go right and the things that go wrong. This involves paying attention to *what is taught*, to *the needs and reactions of the class both as individuals and as a group*, and to *one's own behaviour*. We can stimulate our thinking in each of these three areas by asking ourselves questions such as the following.

What is taught

I have emphasized at a number of points throughout the book that what is taught should be relevant, and I offered a definition of the term. But what do you understand by relevance? Think about your own experiences as a student and as a child in school. What kind of things in your studies appeared to you to have relevance and why? Similarly, what kind of things appeared to be irrelevant and why?

Once you have answered these points, think about the term *interesting*. Are things which are relevant necessarily interesting? Is there any real difference between the two terms, and if so what is the difference? *Relevance* does not simply mean that something is seen to be helpful in preparing you for a job when you finish studying. It can also be helpful in enabling you to relate more satisfactorily to others or to make better use of leisure time, or in fathoming out the meaning of life.

Think for a moment about the school curriculum, whether at primary school or secondary school level. Setting aside for a moment your own preferences, what areas of it would appear to have most relevance to children growing up in today's world? What areas of the curriculum seem to be there simply out of tradition?

Then think about the methods we use to teach the curriculum. What do these methods owe to tradition and to fixed patterns of thinking? How can we change these methods? Why is it, for example, that even slow learning children have no difficulty in remembering detailed facts associated with their favourite pop groups or sports stars, whereas they seem unable to assimilate the material we try to teach in class? Does the fault lie in the material? Or in the methods we use to teach it? Or in something else?

Now think for a moment about your own chosen or preferred teaching subject. What areas of this are relevant to today's children? What teaching methods are most likely to bring out this relevance? If children find the subject uninteresting why is this? If they fail to develop your own love for the subject in spite of your best efforts who or what (if anything) is to blame?

Finally think about methods of examination and assessment. What is the real point of assessment? Does it help the learning process? Does it help develop a love for the subject? If you are doubtful about the value of assessment, how could we improve upon present practices? Do public examinations, by whatever name we choose to call them, have a place, and if so what is that place?

In thinking about each of the above questions, you will probably have emphasized to yourself the extent to which the material we teach in schools is closely linked to the issue of class control. Children who are interested and motivated tend to produce few control problems, while those who are bored and frustrated produce any number. The more you can think about ways of using the curriculum to interest and motivate children, therefore, the less you will have to concern yourself with problems of control.

The needs and reactions of the class

Each child is an individual. Make a list of those factors within the individual that are likely to make for a co-operative member of the class and those factors that are likely to prompt trouble-making. Some of the factors on your list should be to do with ability, while others will be to do with background and experience, and others will be to do with personality. All these various factors will interact with and influence each other. Think about the way in which this interaction and influence takes place. Use your own life experiences as an example. How have the various instances of academic failure (even poor marks on unimportant tests) which you may have encountered influenced your outlook? Have you generally experienced encouragement from your parents and family? What would have been the result had this encouragement not been there? What factors of personality have influenced the way in which you have tackled academic work and related to your teachers? Have you felt impatient and frustrated at times, and has it been possible to control these feelings? How have you responded when teachers have treated you unfairly? Or when you felt they have failed you in some way or been inadequate at their job? What qualities in you have made it easy for you to relate to certain teachers and hard to relate to others? Has it been possible for you to develop or change these qualities in any way over the years?

Now try and relate the answers to the above questions to children. Many of them will not have had the advantages in life that you have had. Who if anyone is to blame for this? Is it the child? If you were in his or her position, what would you want from teachers in order to remedy your disadvantage? Would you know how to ask for this help? And how would you feel and react if teachers refused this help or failed to recognize your need for it? How would you feel and how would you react if your marks were always at or near the bottom of the class and if most of the work offered in class was outside your understanding?

Think next about the way in which children show their feelings and their needs. There is a great variety here. How do you recognize whether individual children are interested in their work or not? How do you recognize when they are bored or frustrated? How do you recognize whether they are hurt by failure or encouraged by success? Are there differences in this respect between the sexes and with children of different ages? How do you recognize personality characteristics such as extraversion and introversion in children? How do you recognize a particularly anxious child? What is the best way to encourage individual children to discuss their feelings and their problems with you? Why do some children find it much easier to enter into such discussion than do others?

Now consider the group behaviour of children. Why is it that some classes are easy to teach and others more difficult? Why is it that this is often the case even when the two classes are of parallel ability? What are the qualities that make children stars and leaders within the class and how can you recognize these qualities? What can you do to form good relationships with these children and to obtain their co-operation? Why is it necessary to protect the self-esteem of stars and leaders and indeed of all class members? How can such protection best be undertaken? What is likely to happen if children have their self-esteem threatened by your actions or by the nature of the work that they are given to do?

Within any class, sub-groups are likely to form, and these can have a significant influence upon relationships within the class and upon class control. List some of the factors that can lead to the formation of these sub-groups, and give some thought to the nature of these various groups. In what way are they likely to pose problems of class control? How can the teacher best go about the task of relating successfully to the different groups and ensuring that they co-operate in class? Which sub-groups would you personally prefer to work with? Some teachers enjoy the challenge of working with less conformist sub-groups while others prefer working with those who identify fully with the ethos and practices of the school. Can you say why sub-groups of a particular kind appeal to you more than do others?

Why is it that the behaviour of individual children is often different when they are with a group from when they are on their own? What can be done to prevent children from developing negative behaviours when they are with a group who pose problems of class control? Conversely, how can you best enlist the co-operation of the group in helping a child who is outside the group and who is causing trouble? And what can be done to prevent an easily led group from admiring and trying to copy the behaviour of a deviant member of the class?

Finally think back to your own membership of various sub-groups when you were in school. What attracted you to these groups and why did you give them your loyalty? To what extent did the groups help you in your school progress and to what extent do you feel they acted as a hindrance? Did you sometimes find yourself acting out of character in order to make yourself acceptable to the group, and did this sometimes cause you to pose your teachers specific problems of class control? Thinking back to your own experiences, does this help you to understand the behaviour of individuals and sub-groups within the classes that you teach? What sort of approach from the teacher do you think would have been most effective with you as a child and with the sub-groups of which you were a member? Did any teacher employ this approach and if so what sort of personality characteristics did he or she have? Was the teacher popular with you and with your sub-groups, and if so why was this?

Your own behaviour

Following directly on from the last point, do you think you have the characteristics of the teacher we have just been thinking about? If he or she had qualities you admire, can you develop or further develop these in yourself? Now make a list of the qualities you actively disliked in the teachers you worked with. Why did you dislike these qualities? Do you feel to have any of them yourself? If so, can you gradually work to eliminate them? If you are in doubt as to whether you have these qualities or not (and the good qualities mentioned above) talk to a friend who knows you well and ask him or her to rate you on them. You can do the same for your friend. Be honest with each other and use the exercise as a way towards greater self-understanding.

Now carry out the same exercise, but instead of thinking back to teachers you liked and disliked think back to someone who was good at class control and someone who was ineffective. What respective qualities seemed to be involved in this good and bad control? Again analyse yourself with the help of a friend and try to determine the degree to which you have these sets of qualities and what you can do to develop or eliminate them as appropriate. I mentioned in Chapter 6 the possibility of video or audio taping your performance in front of a real or imagined class and analysing the results. If you don't have access to the necessary equipment, stand in front of a full-length mirror and address yourself as if you were talking to a class (if this exercise makes you feel uncomfortable ask yourself why). How would you feel as a child in school if you were being addressed in this way? How would you want to react to the person concerned? Children are often quite shrewd in summing up a teacher even on first acquaintance. How would you sum yourself up if the image in the mirror was that of a stranger? This exercise is not as hard to do as it sounds. Initially your image in the mirror will look very familiar and you will find it impossible to think of it as anybody but yourself. However, after persevering for a short time a sudden shift in focus often takes place and the image will seem curiously remote and impersonal.

Now reread Chapter 8 and the points raised there on the management of your own emotions. When you have done this, make a list first of the child behaviours that make you fearful in your dealings with problems of class control, and second of the behaviours that make you angry.Take your time over these lists and be completely honest with yourself. These lists are not there to make you feel impatient or ashamed of yourself but simply to help you in the future. Now rewrite each list in the form of a hierarchy, with the most important items of behaviour at the top and the least important at the bottom.

At this stage, it is a great advantage if you are working with a friend or with a group of student or serving teachers, because this allows a degree of role-playing to take place. The basic role-playing exercise is as follows, but you will be able to think of useful variants of it.

> Take an item from one of the lists you have just compiled. It is usually easier if you start with a relatively non-stressful item and then work up the list. Write down an imaginary or a remembered classroom situation that incorporates the item of child behaviour concerned, and then give it to the friend or colleague with whom you are working. He or she is given time to think about it, and then takes the role of the child and acts out the situation with you, while you take the role of the teacher and experiment with behaviours that appear to be effective and that allow you to remain calm and composed. If you are working in a group and other colleagues are therefore watching your performance they can be invited to comment constructively at the end.

If there are situations rather than child behaviours that you find threatening (for example, interruptions in the middle of your lesson, or discovering that you have brought the wrong text book or that some item of equipment fails to work) these can also be incorporated into role-play exercises. Should you be working on your own with no opportunity for role-playing, then substitute visual imagery instead. Picture the classroom confrontation to yourself in clear detail, acting out your own role in your mind and observing yourself remaining collected and in control. If you feel anger or anxiety beginning to arise, break off the exercise, wait until the feeling has dissipated, then start again from the beginning. Gradually the mind will become habituated to the imaginary scene, and when it occurs in reality something of the composed reaction that has become apparent in working through this exercise will remain. Don't expect rapid and dramatic results. Progress will be gradual, but over a period of time you will notice unmistakable results.

Role-playing and visualization are not the only ways in which you can make use of the lists you have just drawn up, however. Go through each one carefully and see what can be done to *avoid* the confrontations or stressful situations which the lists identify. Don't feel this is being cowardly or avoiding the issue. It is simply using your professional skills to avoid unnecessary problems, and I have drawn attention to the importance of this throughout the book. Ask yourself, 'Would more careful planning of my lessons or of certain areas of them be of help?'. 'Would a little extra time spent checking and familiarizing myself with items of equipment avoid embarrassing or threatening situations?'. 'Would it be possible to enlist the help of the children rather more, perhaps by asking two or three of them to check over the equipment with me during break or lunchtime so that I can call upon them during the lesson?'. 'Can I give more responsibilities and more opportunities to my more troublesome children, so that they can identify more with the success of my lessons?'. 'Are there occasions when I should seek to talk to individual children on their own rather than risk a confrontation with them in class?'. 'Is there a better way to tackle problems such as failure to give in homework, perhaps by talking the whole thing through with the class and agreeing with them on reasonable expectations and on the sanctions to be applied when work comes in late?'.

Now make another list, this time of all the happenings in class that leave you with a good feeling. What is it that makes them successful? Without worrying about sounding egotistical, write down those qualities and behaviours in yourself that seem to contribute to this success. Some of them will be to do with planning and presentation of lesson material, others will be to do with you as a person. How can you further develop these various strengths? Why is it that you are not always able to bring out these good points in your work and in yourself when you are in front of a class? What can be done about it? Are you allowing experiences outside the classroom (your moods and so on) to get in the way of the good work that you know you can do? Which children and which parts of your own teaching subject or subjects bring out the best in you and why? How can you generalize this 'best' so that it becomes the response to other children and to other parts of your work as well? If you actively dislike some children and some aspects of your teaching duties, why is this so and what can be done about it? But remember not to use your list of your good points simply as a method of self-criticism. It should help to reassure you that you have reasons to commend yourself as a teacher. You are offering something of value to your children, and you already have important areas of class control very much in your command. All that is now needed is a steady and thoughtful extension of these areas, and this extension will come with further practice and experience.

Specific strategies

Having given thought to the three main variables in class control (the curriculum, the children and the teacher) next consider how you might operate specific strategies to deal with class control problems which have already arisen. As a first step, write out the precise behaviours both in individuals and in a class which in your judgement or experience represent active control problems. Arrange them in a hierarchy, going from major problems at the top to minor problems at the bottom.

Now give thought to the possible causes of these problems and to the way in which you (or other teachers you have observed) normally respond to them. Making reference to Chapters 1 to 3, decide whether your analyses of the causes appear to be appropriate, and by making reference to Chapters 4 and 5 decide whether normal responses appear to be effective. In the light of the causes which you are now able to identify, what responses appear to you to stand most chance of success? You may find it helpful to sketch out a full response programme, perhaps in the form of a behaviour modification schedule. Select one of the items of behaviour at the bottom end of your hierarchy and make a start on this first. If the behaviour modification approach is in your view unsuitable in this instance, design a cognitive approach instead. Either way, make sure your approach is thoroughly practical. It must state unequivocally what you actually propose to do in the face of the child or class behaviours concerned. Now list the possible child or class responses to your actions. Remember that I stressed the good teacher is always prepared. Class control problems are far more likely to persist if the teacher is constantly being surprised and caught out by the children's behaviour. Children are only too capable of the unexpected, so widen your range of expectations. If a child produces behaviour A and you respond to it with behaviour B, what could happen next? You may be hoping for behaviour C, but what if the child tries behaviour D or E ? Will you know what to do? Or will you be at a loss and either lose valuable time in thinking or come out with something disastrous like a wild (or much too feeble) threat? Time spent running over possible eventualities in your own mind or in a group discussion with other student or serving teachers helps ensure you have the flexibility to deal with whatever comes up. Better still, talk things over, if possible, with a group of children. Be careful to work only with a small group, and be sure you pick an opportunity when they are in a co-operative frame of mind and eager for a discussion session on an interesting topic. Often such opportunities arise quite readily during teaching practice.

Start by explaining frankly to the class that relationships between teachers and children are of great importance if school is to run smoothly, but that often (as in the world outside) relationships are soured because people misunderstand each other and misinterpret what the other is trying to do or say. Then throw things open by asking them what they expect of a teacher and what they are prepared to offer in return. By degrees the discussion can be steered towards a debate on why children misbehave in class and what kinds of teacher response are most likely to put things right. Children are usually very frank and open in this kind of debate, particularly if they feel the teacher is being frank and open with them in return. They may even comment, perceptively and helpfully, upon your own classroom performance, and you would do well to learn from these comments while at the same time treating them lightheartedly and pointing out that no one is perfect.

Discussions of this kind, and discussions with colleagues and friends, should also help clarify the position on rewards and punishments. What rewards and punishments are likely to be effective and why? How does their nature change as one moves across the age-groups and the ability levels? What are the dangers attendant upon rewards and particularly upon punishments? How can these dangers best be avoided? How necessary is it for a school to have a common policy upon such matters, and how should this policy be determined? What happens when children ignore punishments or otherwise demonstrate their ineffectiveness?

Colleagues and the school itself

When discussing with colleagues, it is also vital to think about ways in which teachers can help each other. Would you know how to ask a colleague for help? What would you do if the position were reversed and the colleague came to you for assistance? Or if he or she came to you and offered help without being asked? Would you see this as a form of implicit criticism of you? Would you feel offended or grateful?

Closely linked to these points, how do you think a school should be organized to minimize control problems and to deal with those that may happen to arise? What should the chain of authority and management be within the school from the headteacher downwards, and what kind of relationship should the school seek to have with its pupils? Think of a good school in your own experience and then compare it with one less good. Try if possible to select two schools with similar catchment areas. Why is one school better than the other? Is it to do with the headteacher? The staff? The school buildings and layout? School organization? School rules? School ethos and climate? Or a combination of these things plus other factors you can identify? What are the outside constraints upon a school that may make it harder for the headteacher and staff to deal with control problems? Can the school do anything about these constraints, and what should its relationship in the context of these problems be with parents and the community?

Your personal professional philosophy

Finally, think carefully about your own professional philosophy. What kind of teacher do you want to become? Don't be afraid to be idealistic, but temper your idealism with realism. How do you want your relationship with your children to develop? Obviously you want to be liked and respected, but what do these terms mean in your own case? How are you going to recognize this liking and respect and how are you going to earn it? Clearly you want to have good class control, but do you want to be thought of as a strict disciplinarian or as a kindly and approachable person? Dependent upon your answer, what qualities do you have that may make you a disciplinarian or someone who is approachable? How will you cope with the frustrations and disappointments that may lie between you and your chosen role?

These questions go fairly deep and relate to the person you really are and to your reasons for entering the teaching profession. Only you can answer them. But it is the willingness to appraise your own behaviour whenever necessary, and to grow and develop, that will help you make a success of your teaching. I wish you well.

Further reading

This book is one of a series of practical texts, and it is not intended that it be sprinkled with references or further reading. Nevertheless, you may wish to gain additional background in some of the areas which it covers, and the following may be of some help.

Fontana, D. (1981) *Psychology for Teachers*. Leicester: The British Psychological Society and Macmillan Press.
One is always very diffident about recommending one's own books, but this book sets out to cover the main lessons that the teacher can learn from a study of psychology, and links in with many of the themes in the present text.

Fontana, D. (ed.) (1984) *Behaviourism and Learning Theory in Education*. Edinburgh: Scottish Academic Press.
As I only edited this book I don't feel so badly about recommending it. There are chapters covering all aspects of behaviour modification, the token economy, precision teaching and related issues.

Howe, M.J.A. (1984) *Psychology of Learning*. Oxford: Basil Blackwell.
This is an excellent short book on the cognitive approach. Though it does not aim to deal specifically with class control issues, it is full of information on how best to understand and guide children and gain their classroom co-operation.

Galloway, D. (1985) *Schools, Pupils and Special Educational Needs*. London: Croom Helm.
This looks closely at the ways in which schools can be organized and administered so as to cater for the needs of children with special difficulties. A thought-provoking and realistic book, especially strong on the provision of pastoral care.

Laslett, R. and Smith, C. (1983) *Effective Classroom Management*. London: Croom Helm.
A practical and readable guide to managing and administering a classroom so as to lessen the incidence of control problems.

Bloom, B.S. (1982) *Human Characteristics and School Learning*. New York: McGraw Hill.
Perhaps the best short book currently available on how to present school experiences to children in a way which maximizes the chances of success for each one of them.

INDEX